I0758371

How To Apply For Unemployment

Your Strategic Guide to Maximizing Unemployment Benefits

Kaitlin Henderson

Copyright

No part of this book may be reproduced, stored in a retrieval system, or transmitted in any form or by any means, electronic, mechanical, photocopying, recording, scanning, or otherwise, except as permitted under Section 107 or 108 of the 1976 United States Copyright Act, without the prior written permission of the publisher.

This book is protected under the copyright laws of the United States of America. Any reproduction or unauthorized use of the material or artwork contained herein is prohibited without the express written consent of the publisher.

This book is intended solely for informational and educational purposes. It should not be used as a substitute for professional, financial, or legal advice. The author and publisher make no representations or warranties of any kind, express or implied, about the book's completeness, accuracy, reliability, suitability, or availability or the information, products, services, or related graphics contained in the book for any purpose. Therefore, any reliance placed on such information is strictly at your own risk.

Please consult with a professional advisor or attorney before making any financial decisions based on the content of this book. The author and publisher are not responsible for errors, inaccuracies, or omissions. They shall not be liable for any loss or damage of any kind, including, but not limited to, any direct, indirect, incidental, consequential, special, or exemplary damages arising from or in connection with the use of this book or its information.

Printed in the United States of America

Copyright © 2023 By Kaitlin Henderson.

All rights reserved.

Why Should You Read This Book

Kaitlin Henderson is an internationally acclaimed and bestselling personal finance author, lecturer, and advisor. Through her work, she is dedicated to teaching people to manage their money better and to successfully direct their own investments.

Kaitlin is a former management consultant to businesses for which she helped improve operations and profitability. Before, during, and after her time of working crazy hours and traveling too much, she had the good sense to focus on financial matters.

She has spent more than three decades working in various capacities in the financial markets. Kaitlin first invested in mutual funds back in the mid-1980s, when she opened a mutual fund account at Fidelity With the assistance of Dr. Martin Zweig, a well-known analyst of the financial markets.

In addition to investing in securities over the decades, Kaitlin has also successfully invested in real estate and started and managed her own business. She has offered advice to thousands of clients on a range of investment conundrums and concerns.

she earned a Bachelor's Degree in Economics at Yale and an MBA at the Stanford Graduate School of Business. Despite these impediments to lucid reasoning, she came to her senses and decided that life was too short to spend it working long hours and waiting in airports for the benefit of larger companies.

An accomplished freelance personal finance writer, Kaitlin work has been featured and quoted in hundreds of national and local publications, including Kiplinger's Personal Finance Magazine, Los Angeles Times, Chicago Tribune, Bottom Line/Personal, The Wall Street Journal, ABC, CNBC, PBS's Nightly Business Report, FOX, CNN, CBS national radio, Bloomberg Business Radio, National Public Radio, and Business Radio Network. she's also been a featured speaker at a White House conference on retirement planning.

To stay in tune with what real people care about and struggle with Kaitlin still maintains a financial counseling practice.

Table of Contents

Introduction

Alex was a driven individual who lived in the vibrant city of Brooksville, Florida, where hopes and the harsh realities of unstable economic conditions sometimes intersected. Following years of commitment to a business that regrettably folded due to financial instability, Alex was faced with the terrifying possibility of losing his job. Weeks stretched into months as Alex navigated the maze of job applications and interviews. He was disoriented and demoralized by the employment market, which appeared to be an unending labyrinth. Anxiety was palpable, and bills were piling up. It was during this difficult period that Alex and I met, a ray of hope that would transform his life.

My new guide, "How to Apply for Unemployment: Your Strategic Guide to Maximizing Unemployment Benefits," is ready for review. I recently finished the manuscript. This literary treasure offers a roadmap for achieving financial resilience in addition to advice. I told Alex about what he was going through, and then I showed him. Alex was intrigued and turned to the pages, where he discovered not just a guide to managing bureaucratic procedures but also a path to a safer, better future.

The document outlined a methodical procedure for submitting an unemployment insurance claim. It was a holistic approach to optimizing the available support during difficult times, not just about submitting documents. The paper outlined a strategy that went beyond survival; rather, it was a roadmap for thriving in the face of uncertainty, from figuring out qualifying requirements to maximizing pay.

Alex started to change as he immersed himself in useful advice and thoughts. He began to view unemployment as a chance for financial reinvention rather than as a dead end. Equipped with the insights gained from the text, Alex deftly maneuvered through the jobless terrain, making well-informed choices that would ultimately determine his financial trajectory.

The breakthrough occurred earlier than anticipated. By following the advice in the manuscript, Alex was able to find untapped sources of income development in addition to securing his unemployment benefits. The manuscript's strategic strategy served as a model for a victorious resurgence. News of Alex's victory went viral in Brooksville, Florida. Friends, relatives, and even strangers found inspiration in the amazing recovery. The demand for the manuscript, "How to Apply for Unemployment," increased dramatically as it became a popular topic of discussion. People wanted the same leadership that had enabled Alex to overcome hardship and turn it to his advantage. That's what gave rise to the finished book's publication.

"How to Apply for Unemployment" became more than just a book in a world where financial uncertainty is an unpleasant reality; it became a ray of hope for people who are experiencing career setbacks. My thoughtful analysis and methodical approach made it an essential read for anyone attempting to deal with the difficulties of unemployment.

Success tales emanating from this strategic guide reverberated throughout Brooksville, Florida, and beyond, making it a literary gem that any jobless person yearned to own. After all, "How to Apply for Unemployment" acted as a beacon of hope, urging readers to pursue opportunities as they made the transition from financial instability to financial resilience.

At the core of this work lies a purpose that extends far beyond the mere acquisition of unemployment benefits. It is a purpose born from the understanding that our response to adversity shapes not only our immediate circumstances but also our long-term trajectory. As an author deeply influenced by Covey's philosophy, my aim is to illuminate the path not just to financial stability but to a profound transformation of self.

Consider this not as a manual, but as a dialogue—a conversation between kindred spirits navigating the uncharted territories of unemployment. It's a testament to the belief that within every challenge lies an opportunity for growth and empowerment. In crafting this guide, I have endeavored to infuse Covey's principles into the very fabric of our journey, unveiling a strategic approach that transcends the bureaucratic nuances of unemployment applications.

The first step on this journey is a mental shift—a recalibration of how we perceive unemployment. It's easy to view it solely as a period of financial strain, but through the lens of strategic thinking, it becomes a canvas upon which we can paint the portrait of our future selves. Covey's foundational principle of "Begin with the End in Mind" is our compass, urging us to envision not just the end of unemployment but the person we aspire to become through this process.

As we delve into the strategic intricacies of applying for unemployment benefits, we concurrently explore the development of habits that align with Covey's timeless wisdom. The pursuit of benefits becomes an opportunity to cultivate habits of proactivity, prioritization, and effective communication. It's not merely about filling out forms; it's about the disciplined execution of habits that lay the groundwork for a resilient and empowered future.

In the pages that follow, you'll encounter insights and reflections inspired by Covey's principle of "Seek First to Understand, Then to

Be Understood." We navigate the complexities of unemployment not only by understanding the bureaucratic maze but also by understanding ourselves—our strengths, values, and aspirations. This self-awareness becomes the cornerstone upon which we construct a strategy that not only secures benefits but propels us towards a more fulfilling professional trajectory.

The concept of the "Emotional Bank Account," a term coined by Covey, finds resonance in the narrative of our unemployment journey. How we navigate the emotional challenges, both within ourselves and in our interactions with others, significantly influences the balance of our emotional bank account. By investing in empathy, effective communication, and resilience, we enrich our emotional capital, fostering healthier relationships and a more robust sense of self.

This guide isn't a guarantee of a painless journey through unemployment; rather, it's an assurance that, armed with strategic thinking and Covey's principles, you possess the tools to navigate the challenges with grace and purpose. It is an acknowledgment that, in the face of uncertainty, our response is a choice—a choice to be proactive, to prioritize what truly matters, and to use this period as a crucible for personal and professional transformation.

In the spirit of Covey's "Sharpen the Saw," we explore not only the practical aspects of benefit applications but also the holistic well-being that sustains us throughout this process. Strategies for maintaining physical, mental, and emotional well-being intertwine with the overarching narrative, recognizing that a resilient self is better equipped to weather the storms of change.

As you immerse yourself in the chapters ahead, envision this guide not as a solitary journey but as a collaborative exploration. Consider me not just an author but a fellow traveler, sharing insights and wisdom gleaned from both personal experiences and the profound teachings of Stephen R. Covey. Together, let us transcend the limitations of unemployment, transforming it from a mere chapter in our lives to a pivotal turning point—one where we emerge not just beneficiaries of a system but architects of our destinies.

May this guide serve as a beacon of empowerment, illuminating the path to not only claiming unemployment benefits but to claiming a future defined by resilience, purpose, and the unwavering belief that, in every challenge, there lies an opportunity for greatness. Welcome to a journey of strategic transformation—welcome to "How to Apply for Unemployment: Your Strategic Guide to Maximizing Unemployment Benefits."

Chapter 1

Understanding Unemployment

Globally, unemployment is a widespread and complicated problem that impacts people, families, and entire economies. Unemployment has far-reaching effects on mental health, social stability, and general well-being in addition to financial difficulties. In this article, we shall examine the causes, effects, and possible remedies of unemployment as we explore its complex character.

What Is Unemployment?

The situation of not having a job, despite actively seeking one, is sometimes referred to as unemployment. Economists frequently distinguish between several forms of unemployment, including cyclical, structural, and frictional. People who are between jobs or entering the labor force for the first time are said to be experiencing frictional unemployment. Economic shifts, such as the obsolescence of some skills due to technological improvements, are the root cause of structural unemployment. Conversely, cyclical unemployment is tied to the economic cycle, increasing during recessions and decreasing during expansions.

Six Types of Unemployment

Frictional Unemployment: The Essential Shift

A common belief is that frictional unemployment is an inevitable and natural part of any dynamic economy. It happens to people who are changing careers or are joining the labor for the first time. These job searchers are usually in the process of locating a suitable position, and the lag between positions adds to frictional unemployment.

Changes in personal circumstances, moving to a new place, or consciously leaving one job in quest of other chances can all have an impact on this kind of unemployment. Frictional unemployment often has a brief duration and is frequently caused by a delay in the hiring of suitable candidates and the availability of positions.

Structural Unemployment: Changing Workplace Foundations

When an economy undergoes significant structural changes that make particular occupational roles or skill sets outdated, structural unemployment results. This kind of unemployment is strongly linked to changes in consumer tastes, the state of the global economy, and technological improvements.

Automation and technological advancements, for instance, have the potential to create structural unemployment if machines or artificial intelligence replace traditional labor. Structural unemployment may also result from industries that are declining as a result of globalization or changes in consumer demand, trapping people with specialized skills in a labor market that no longer needs them.

Proactive measures like retraining programs, education campaigns, and regulations meant to ease workers' transition from decreasing to developing industries are often necessary to address structural unemployment.

Cycling Unemployment: Following the Trends in the Economy

Intimately linked to the economic cycle, cyclical unemployment rises during recessions and falls during expansions. This kind of unemployment is a direct result of changes in an economy's aggregate demand.

Businesses may reduce expenses during a recession or economic contraction, which could result in layoffs and an increase in cyclical unemployment. On the other hand, during times of economic expansion, companies add more employees to satisfy the rising demand, which lowers the rate of cyclical unemployment.

Implementing macroeconomic policies, such as fiscal and monetary measures, to boost economic growth during downturns or restrict it during expansions is a common step in understanding and managing cyclical unemployment.

Additional Types of Unemployment

Although the main forms of unemployment are structural, cyclical, and frictional, other categories highlight particular situations or traits of unemployment:

Seasonal Unemployment: Occurs when some jobs have a seasonal demand, which results in off-season jobless periods. Workers in retail or agriculture throughout the non-holiday seasons are two examples.

Underemployment: While not the same as unemployed, underemployment is the state in which people work in jobs that do not completely make use of their abilities, credentials, or availability. Part-time work, temporary jobs, or occupations that don't fit a person's skill set can all lead to this kind of predicament.

Hidden unemployment: The term "hidden unemployment" describes those who would take a job offer even if they are not actively looking for one. These people might not be included in official unemployment figures, giving us a more complex picture of the job market.

The complexities of unemployment go beyond the general term to include a range of forms influenced by sociological, technological, and economic factors. A foundation for comprehending the various aspects of unemployment is provided by frictional, structural, and cyclical unemployment, while other categories highlight particular situations within the labor market.

Understanding the many forms of unemployment is crucial for economists, policymakers, and people in general. It enables the creation of focused plans to deal with the underlying causes of unemployment, whether via training programs, educational initiatives, or macroeconomic regulations. Through a thorough comprehension of the various definitions and forms of unemployment, communities may strive to cultivate flexible and resilient labor markets that support long-term economic expansion and offer significant career prospects to everybody.

Reasons for Unemployment

Technological Advancements: As automation and artificial intelligence replace some work that people have historically performed by hand, the quick speed of technological innovation may result in employment displacement. Even if these developments increase productivity, those with outdated skills may find it difficult to obtain new jobs, leading to structural unemployment.

Globalization: Higher labor costs in industrialized nations may result in job losses in some industries due to increased international trade and outsourcing. The relocation of workers to nations with cheaper production costs may cause structural unemployment when industries in some places collapse.

Economic Recessions: Companies may save expenses by hiring fewer people or downsizing during a recession, raising the rate of cyclical unemployment. This kind of unemployment can be especially severe during financial crises and is closely linked to the business cycle.

Mismatch of Skills: Shifts in the economy may result in a mismatch between the skills that businesses require and the talents that workers possess. Some people may experience extended periods of unemployment due to this structural problem, particularly if they lack the skills required for the occupations that are currently available.

Labor Market Policies: Laws pertaining to the minimum wage and employment restrictions, for example, have the potential to affect the rate of unemployment. Although the goal of these regulations is worker protection, they may also make it difficult for some people to enter the workforce, thus raising the unemployment rate.

Unemployment Economic Impact on Individuals and Society

The social science of economics, which examines the production, distribution, and consumption of goods and services, has a significant impact on how people live their lives and how communities are constructed. The economic impact is extensive, affecting everything from individual financial situations to the general well-being of entire communities, both at the micro and macro levels. We shall examine the various ways that economic forces affect people and society as a whole in this article.

Individuals' Microeconomic Impact

Jobs and earnings

Employment and income have one of the most direct and immediate effects on the economy at the individual level. An individual's level of life is directly impacted by the number of employment available and the pay paid, which in turn affects access to needs like housing, healthcare, and education. Financial problems can be experienced by individuals and their families as a result of job losses, salary stagnation, or underemployment during economic downturns.

Inequality and Poverty

Societal levels of poverty and income disparity are mostly influenced by economic factors. Systemic hurdles, unequal wealth distribution, and a lack of economic opportunity can keep people in poverty cycles and even entire communities. To solve these problems and achieve a more equitable allocation of resources, a comprehensive strategy combining social and economic policies is needed.

Learning and Development of Skills

Skills development and educational possibilities are shaped by economic considerations. Financial resources frequently determine an individual's access to high-quality education, which affects their capacity to develop the skills that employers are looking for. Differences in access to education can exacerbate social inequality by impeding economic advancement and limiting prospects for upward mobility.

Wellness and Health

People's general well-being and health are closely related to their economic situation. Health disparities may arise from limited access to healthcare, which may be influenced by financial variables such as employment-based insurance. Economic pressures like Unemployment or unstable finances can also exacerbate mental health problems, resulting in a complex interaction between the state of the economy and people's wellbeing.

The Social Effects of Macroeconomics

GDP (gross domestic product) and economic expansion

At the community level, economic growth and the Gross Domestic Product (GDP) are common measures of economic health. The GDP gives information on the total worth of goods and services generated in a nation and can be used to gauge its overall economic output. A country's wealth and the standard of life of its people are largely determined by its economic growth, which is indicated by the GDP's gradual increase.

Rates of Unemployment

Excessive Unemployment can have far-reaching effects on society, impacting not just individuals but also the social fabric as a whole. It causes social discontent, mental health problems, and increasing financial burden. During economic downturns, governments and politicians typically use unemployment rates as a gauge for the state of the economy and devise plans to boost job creation.

Both Deflation and Inflation

The dynamics of inflation and deflation have an effect on people's purchasing power and the stability of pricing in a community. Since moderate inflation reflects rising demand for goods and services, it is frequently seen as a sign of a robust economy. On the other hand, hyperinflation can cause economic instability by devaluing money. Conversely, deflation—a prolonged drop in the overall level of prices—can discourage investment and expenditure and provide a unique set of difficulties.

Public Facilities and Services

The state of the economy affects governments' capacity to spend on infrastructure and deliver basic public services. Public services like healthcare, education, and public safety are funded by tax revenues, which are based on economic activity. Governments may experience financial difficulties during recessions, which could affect the standard and accessibility of public services.

The Relationship Between Macroeconomic and Microeconomic Factors

The macroeconomic and microeconomic facets are closely related, creating a precarious equilibrium that forms the framework of the economy. Financial choices made by individuals, such as saving and spending, affect aggregate demand and ultimately the rate of economic expansion. On the other hand, individual decisions and behaviors are influenced by macroeconomic policies, such as fiscal policies and interest rates.

Consumer Spending Patterns and Confidence

Economic cycles are significantly influenced by consumer confidence, which is a gauge of the public's optimism about the status of the economy. Consumer spending may decline during uncertain economic times, which would lower the demand for products and services. Recessions or other slowdowns in the economy may result from this in turn. On the other hand, economic booms are frequently accompanied by high levels of consumer confidence, which stimulates investment and spending.

Rates of Interest and Borrowing

Interest rates are one instrument that central banks use to control economic activity. Reduced interest rates can encourage borrowing and spending, which will boost the economy. Interest rates have an impact on consumer decisions about credit cards, loans, and mortgages. Conversely, higher interest rates may have a depressing effect on investment and consumption, which may affect both people and companies.

Chapter 2

Why Apply for Unemployment Benefits?

Even the most seasoned professionals may feel trapped in a maze due to unforeseen twists and turns in the constantly shifting employment market. Applying for unemployment benefits is one path that can offer a much-needed lifeline during uncertain economic or personal conditions. We'll solve the puzzles around unemployment benefits in this post, discuss the importance of applying, and give you useful advice for completing the procedure smoothly.

Recognizing the Reasons

When a job is lost, applying for unemployment benefits might not be the first thing that comes to mind, but it's a useful tool meant to offer a financial safety net in trying times. Let's examine some of the main arguments for why filing for unemployment benefits can be a wise and calculated decision.

Assistance with Finances During Transition: Losing a job

frequently triggers a series of financial difficulties. Benefits from unemployment serve as a buffer, providing a short-term source of income while you move jobs. This safety net can relieve short-term financial hardship by helping to pay for necessities like groceries, rent, and bills.

Preserving Balance and Welfare: Losing a job can have an enormous emotional toll that affects both your personal and professional life. Benefits from unemployment insurance give you a sense of security so you can concentrate on looking for your next chance rather than constantly worrying about how you're going to pay your bills.

Investing in Your Job Search: Looking for a job can take a lot of time and resources. Benefits from unemployment insurance provide you with the money to make an investment in your job hunt, such as paying for professional development courses, going to networking functions, or creating an effective CV and cover letter.

Common Challenges and Uncertainties

Even though receiving unemployment benefits seems like a good idea, applying for them can be like navigating a maze. Let's talk about some typical difficulties and unknowns that frequently arise on this path.

How to Get Around the Application Maze: Applying for unemployment benefits can be a complicated procedure with seemingly never-ending paperwork and red tape. It can be difficult to comprehend the criteria and finish the required papers. To make the process simpler, a plethora of government websites and online resources offer step-by-step instructions.

Quality Worries: There is a degree of ambiguity for applicants due to the varying eligibility conditions for unemployment benefits. Your eligibility may be affected by things including the cause of your job loss, the duration of your prior employment, and your availability and capacity for work. Preparing a strong application might be aided by researching and comprehending these requirements in advance.

Stigma Associated with Unemployment: Because of the stigma attached to unemployment, some people can be reluctant to seek benefits. It is imperative to acknowledge that unemployment is a transitory state, and the purpose of benefits is to support people throughout these times of transition.

Useful Advice for Getting Through the Maze of Unemployment

Now that we've discussed the reasons and the difficulties, let's look at some useful advice to help you navigate the maze of unemployment.

Investigate and Comprehend the Eligibility Requirements: Start by doing a comprehensive investigation of the requirements in your area for receiving unemployment benefits. Comprehending the particular prerequisites will aid in ascertaining your eligibility and the necessary paperwork to be ready.

Assemble Documentation Ahead of Time: By assembling the required paperwork in advance, a lot of delays in the application process can be avoided. This could include identification documents, employment verification, and any other documentation the unemployment office requests. Having everything ready makes the application process go more smoothly.

Examine Further Sources: Benefits for unemployment are but one component of the puzzle. Examine further job seekers' resources and help options. Programs run by the government, local associations, and career counseling services can all offer helpful support in different areas of your job hunt.

Create a Support System: Losing your job might be a lonely

experience, but you don't have to go through the maze by yourself. Create a network of friends, family, and job seekers who will support you. Talk about your experiences, give each other advice, and rely on one another for emotional support. Through networking, you may find opportunities and insightful information.

Invest in Skill Development: Make the most of the time you have between employments to advance your skills. Increasing your skill set through online courses, workshops, or certifications might help you stand out as a candidate for jobs. Certain training programs may even be financially supported by some jobless compensation programs.

Remain Upbeat and Determined: Finding a job might be difficult, and obstacles are unavoidable. Remain optimistic and unwavering in the pursuit of your goals. Remember that filing for unemployment benefits is a proactive step toward taking back control of your career path, and acknowledge and celebrate any tiny accomplishments along the process.

Although the idea of losing your job can be like trying to find your way through a maze, filing for unemployment benefits is a calculated step that can offer crucial assistance during times of transition. You can successfully traverse the intricacies of the unemployment process by comprehending the reasons behind things, dealing with typical obstacles, and implementing helpful advice. Accept this chance as a first step toward a more promising and resilient career.

Who Can Apply for Unemployment Benefits

The purpose of this segment is to provide you with useful advice to help you navigate the complexity of the issue of who is eligible to apply for unemployment benefits and to help you make sense of it all.

Recognizing Eligibility

There is no one-size-fits-all solution when it comes to unemployment benefits; eligibility is based on a number of variables. Let's examine the essential elements that establish eligibility for unemployment benefits.

Employment History: Your employment history is one of the main determinants of eligibility. Generally, you have to have worked for a specific amount of time before becoming unemployed to be eligible for unemployment benefits. Location-specific criteria differ, so it's important to find out what the rules are where you live.

Reasons for Quitting One's Job: A big part of deciding your eligibility is what happened when you lost your employment. Most of the time, people who lose their jobs as a result of uncontrollable circumstances, such as layoffs, downsizing, or business closures, qualify for unemployment benefits. Eligibility may be impacted by resignation or termination due to misconduct.

Ability and Availability to Work: You must be able, available, and actively looking for work to be eligible for unemployment benefits. This criterion ensures that benefits go to people who actually want to return to the labor force. When applying for jobs, it's common to be asked to provide documentation of your search activities.

Typical Obstacles and Uncertainties

Getting through the unemployment benefits qualifying requirements can be likened to piecing together a puzzle that has some missing pieces. Let's talk about some of the typical difficulties and questions people have while attempting to find out if they qualify.

Gig Workers and Freelancers: Due to the changing structure of the labor market and the rise in gig and freelance employment, many people are unsure about their eligibility for unemployment benefits. While regular employees usually meet the requirements, freelancers may have different requirements. Look into the laws in your area; some have implemented special initiatives for non-traditional workers.

Part-Time Workers: People who work part-time might be curious about their eligibility for unemployment benefits. Part-time employees may often be eligible, albeit the amount of benefits may vary depending on the number of hours worked and earnings. You can complete the application process more skillfully if you are aware of the subtleties of part-time eligibility.

Self-Employed People and Independent Contractors: When it comes to unemployment compensation, self-employed people and independent contractors confront difficulties. These individuals might not have been qualified in the past, but some areas have made exceptions, particularly in light of the current economic climate. Look into whether any programs that address the needs of independent contractors have been developed in your area.

Practical Tips for Navigating Eligibility

Now that we've discussed the nuances of eligibility, let's look at some useful advice to help you get through the maze of who is eligible for unemployment benefits.

Investigate Local Laws: The requirements for receiving unemployment benefits differ depending on where you live, so start by learning about the laws that apply there. Websites run by the government, job placement services, and legal aid groups can all offer helpful information on qualifying conditions that may be relevant to your situation.

Record Your Employment Background: Maintain thorough records of all the jobs you've had, including the dates you worked there, the reasons you left, and any pertinent paperwork like layoff or termination letters. A thorough record will make the application process go more smoothly and improve your chances of fulfilling the requirements.

Comprehend Particular Situations: If you work in non-traditional employment categories, such as part-time work or freelancing, spend some time learning about the particular qualifying requirements that can apply to you. Keep up with any revisions or modifications to unemployment benefit programs that might be relevant to you or other people in your situation.

Get Ready for the Requirement in the Job Search: The majority of unemployment insurance programs demand that recipients actively look for work. To be ready, keep a record of your job search activities, such as the applications you've filed, the networking gatherings you've attended, and the interviews you've had. By being proactive, you meet eligibility requirements and increase your chances of discovering new opportunities.

Seek Professional Advice: If figuring out the eligibility requirements seems onerous, think about getting advice from experts in the area. You can get information related to your case from career coaches, legal counsellors, or employment counselors, which will help you make an informed decision about filing for unemployment benefits.

Keep Yourself Updated on Changes: Policies and programs pertaining to unemployment benefits are prone to change, creating a dynamic landscape. Keep abreast of any revisions or changes to the eligibility requirements, particularly in reaction to changes in the global economy or other events. You can modify your approach to the application process by being aware of changes.

Remember that, with the correct information and preparation, navigating the maze of eligibility for unemployment benefits is possible when you find yourself at a crossroads of doubt and are unsure of your eligibility. Through comprehension of the elements that affect eligibility, resolution of typical obstacles, and use of useful advice, you can go forward with applying for unemployment benefits with assurance. You'll discover a way to the assistance you require as you make your way through the many turns and turns of your career by navigating the road through the maze.

How To Apply for Unemployment Benefit

Life, with its unexpected twists, weaves intricate threads that sometimes unravel, leading us to confront the uncertainty of unemployment. In the intricate dance of employment and finances, mastering the art of constructing the safety net of unemployment benefits becomes an indispensable skill. This article invites you on a creative expedition through the unemployment benefits application process, breaking it down step-by-step and providing practical and imaginative tips to alleviate the intimidating nature of the journey.

Do Your Research and Compile Data

A stellar unemployment application is akin to a carefully crafted painting, starting with the right colors. Initiate the process by delving into the specific laws and regulations applicable to your area. Utilize online forums, job centers, and government websites for valuable insights. Collect information on required paperwork, qualifying criteria, and any distinctive actions.

Creative Tip: Envision your research as a quest for hidden treasures. Picture yourself exploring the less-traveled corners of the internet, uncovering informational gems that illuminate your creative path.

Revisit Your Work Experience: One Document After Another

Your work history forms the canvas upon which your application will be painted. Ensure a comprehensive file detailing your employment history, encompassing dates of employment, reasons for job departure, and relevant documents such as severance agreements or termination letters.

Creative Tip: Envision your work history as a compelling narrative. Craft a story that accentuates your skills, experiences, and the twists of fate that brought you to this juncture. This narrative not only aids your application but lays the groundwork for your forthcoming professional endeavors.

Write Your Own Symphony: The Method of Application

Now is the time to compose your masterpiece—the application procedure itself. Most regions provide online platforms for filing unemployment claims. Pay meticulous attention to each section, filling it out as directed, as precision is paramount in this creative process.

Creative Tip: Picture the application as a blank canvas awaiting your artistic touch. Thoughtfully paint each component, infusing it with the essence of your unique career journey.

The Challenge Dance: How to Use the Application Maze

The application process resembles a dance, with each dancer encountering stumbling blocks. Common challenges include navigating complex forms, understanding legal jargon, and ensuring your application stands out. Break down the steps, seek assistance when needed, and approach the process with the dexterity of a professional dancer.

Creative Tip: Think of the challenges as dance steps. Embrace each one with the grace of a dancer executing a complex routine. Enlist the help of friends, family, or online communities to create a collective dance, making the process more enjoyable.

Face the Dragon: Resolving Eligibility Issues

Eligibility requirements may sometimes seem like a mythical dragon guarding the gates. Equip yourself with knowledge and confront the dragon head-on. Understand the specific regulations in your area, and if uncertainty arises, seek guidance from legal experts or employment counselors.

Creative Tip: Envision eligibility criteria as a mythical quest. Armed with determination and a wealth of information, you, the valiant explorer, embark on a quest to conquer the dragon and claim the valuable treasure of unemployment benefits.

Bringing Your Symphony Together: Confirmation and Follow-Up

After composing your application symphony, verification and follow-up serve as the grand finale. Some applications may require additional paperwork or verification steps. Be proactive in providing requested information and regularly check the progress of your application.

Creative Tip: Visualize the verification process as a musical crescendo. Each document submitted contributes to the harmonious melody of your application's success, much like a note in a symphony.

Effective and Creative Success Suggestions

Unemployment benefits are just one color on your canvas. Explore additional resources and assistance programs available to job seekers. Government initiatives, community associations, and online platforms offer numerous opportunities to enhance your skills and broaden your professional palette.

Creative Tip: Consider these additional resources as wellsprings of inspiration for your artwork. Each resource adds complexity and richness to your professional experience, akin to a painter discovering new techniques or a musician learning new instruments.

Create a Signature to Make Your Job Search Unique

While unemployment benefits provide a financial safety net, your job search is an unfinished masterpiece. Personalize your job search by exploring positions that align with your interests, abilities, and career goals. Think of it as adding your signature to the canvas of your career.

Creative Tip: Your job search is the signature brushstroke on your canvas. Investigate opportunities that resonate with your unique style, creating a signature masterpiece that reflects your authentic self.

Create a Positive Melody: Sustaining an Upbeat Attitude

The artistic process of applying for unemployment benefits can be emotionally taxing. Maintain an optimistic mindset, viewing this period as a creative interlude between professional movements. Celebrate small victories, stay resilient, and keep your creative spirit alive.

Creative Tip: Consider the journey as a joyful symphony. Each challenge overcome is a note in the melody, creating a harmonious soundtrack for your professional resilience.

In Summary

Envision yourself as the artist of your own destiny as you apply for unemployment benefits and embark on a creative journey. From choosing your palette to dancing over the obstacles and composing your application symphony, each step is an opportunity for creativity and self-expression. Infuse your journey with imagination, tenacity, and a dash of creative flair, and witness your masterpiece unfold—a canvas of opportunity and empowerment in the dynamic terrain of your career narrative.

Where To Apply for Unemployment Benefit

Embarking on the quest for the golden door of unemployment benefits is like seeking stability in the intricate maze of employment, especially when the future appears uncertain. This post acts as your treasure map, guiding you through a creative exploration of where to submit an unemployment application. Prepare for an exhilarating journey that blends pragmatism with whimsy as we uncover the locations holding the doors to financial relief.

The Online Platforms as the Digital Oasis

You should begin by investigating the websites that act as entry points to unemployment benefits. The internet world is a vast oasis, offering easily navigable webpages or portals for initiating and completing your application.

Creative Tip: Envision the web platform as a mystical entrance to an online garden. Picture the seeds of your application sprouting into a thriving tree of financial support as you enter your information.

The Knowledge Citadel: Official Websites

Government websites are informational citadels that contain all the data you need to start your search. These websites frequently act as thorough manuals, offering information on qualifying requirements, necessary paperwork, and precise directions on where and how to apply.

Creative Tip: See the official website as an elderly wise man who possesses the key to solving the riddles of unemployment insurance. Examine its pages with curiosity, looking for the knowledge that will lead you on your path.

The Town Square: Neighborhood Job Centers

The town square is a hive of activity, and local job centers are essential to your search for unemployment benefits. Connect with these physical sites or make an online connection to access helpful resources, talk with job counselors, and receive one-on-one help with your application.

Creative Tip: Visualize the job center as a bustling market. Connect with the lively spirit, share your experiences with other explorers, and let the town square's collective knowledge guide you as you pursue your goals.

The Social Grove: Neighborhood Associations

Community groups are the social orchards that foster support and aid. These organizations frequently collaborate with local governments to offer job seekers workshops, additional resources, and counseling. Leverage your community ties to enhance your application process.

Creative Tip: Visualize neighborhood associations as the branches of a pillar of strength. Make an effort to connect with people, and let the strength of the group as a whole provide stability as you navigate the labyrinth of unemployment.

Obstacles on the Way: Using Creativity to Get Through Them

The Magical Forest: The application process for jobless benefits can resemble an enchanted woodland with its maze-like forms and foreign jargon. Use your imagination to tackle this task, breaking down shapes into little, achievable chunks.

Creative Tip: Envision each form as a path-guarding magical creature. By getting to know the species' languages and peculiarities, you can tame them, turning the task into a fun adventure.

The Enigma of Eligibility: Seeking Informed Advice

Understanding eligibility requirements may seem like unraveling mysteries. Consult with career counselors, attorneys, or even internet forums where experienced travelers exchange advice. Consider eligibility as a riddle that needs to be solved using the community's combined knowledge.

Creative Tip: See the requirements for eligibility as a mystic puzzle. Interact with the community to make the voyage more cooperative and pleasurable, much like a group of intrepid travelers combining their knowledge to solve the puzzle.

The Verification Dance: Recording Your Narrative

Keep a record of your career progress to complete the verification dance. Consider this a storytelling dance rather than an assignment. Every document you provide adds to the intricate fabric of your application, acting as a chapter in your story.

Creative Tip: Visualize the process of verification as a dance performance. Present your documents with style, using a ballet of paperwork to captivate the audience (in this case, the application reviewers) and tell the tale of your abilities and experiences.

Effective and Creative Success Suggestions

The Treasure Hunt: Applying for unemployment benefits is just the beginning of your journey toward finding this hidden gem. Investigate the extra resources and assistance that your town has to offer. Consider it as an ongoing treasure hunt where you can find valuable opportunities for career counseling, networking gatherings, and skill-building programs.

Creative Tip: See these materials as undiscovered gems that are just waiting to be found. Approach every class or event with the enthusiasm of someone searching for hidden treasure and discovering important information that will advance your career.

Let your creative juices flow as you set out to apply for unemployment benefits. Imagine the route as a creative trip through social groves, town squares, government citadels, and internet portals. Face obstacles with the ingenuity of a seasoned problem-solver, transforming difficult forms into magical meetings and qualifying requirements into cooperative puzzles. Adorn your job search with the brushstrokes of an artist and embrace the fabric of resources as undiscovered gems. Remember, this is an artistic investigation of your career story, not merely a trip through unemployment. Bring creativity, tenacity, and a dash of whimsy to every step you take, and observe as the opportunities present themselves to you like a blank canvas ready to be painted with the masterpiece of your next career chapter.

Chapter 3

Eligibility Criteria

*What is needed To Apply
for Unemployment*

Embarking on the process of applying for unemployment benefits is akin to preparing for an exhilarating voyage. Picture it as a mission where you, the intrepid adventurer, must gather the necessary information and resources to skillfully navigate the twists and turns of the employment maze. In this imaginative guide, we'll delve into the basics, infusing a touch of whimsy into the procedure, and provide you with a roadmap to discover the hidden gems essential for a successful application.

Your Personal Records

Consider your identity documents as the wizard's grimoire, containing the sorcerous incantations required to open the doors to unemployment benefits. Assemble your driver's license, passport, or other official identification document. This mystical grimoire not only establishes your identity but also unlocks the doors for the upcoming journey.

Creative Tip: Imagine yourself as an apprentice leafing through the wizard's grimoire to locate the ideal spell. Every identity paper is a spell working in concert to unlock the door to financial assistance.

Documentation of Past Employment

Your work history is your time-traveling amulet, enabling you to traverse your career chronology. Gather your W-2 forms, pay stubs, and any other records that demonstrate your work history. This item establishes your eligibility and acts as proof of your contribution to the workforce.

Creative Tip: Envision your work history as a time-traveling amulet with magical properties. Sort through your files and picture the many points in your job journey, like a tapestry that gradually reveals itself as you go through time.

An Extensive Log of Employment Termination

Every explorer needs a scribe to document the story of their expedition. In the realm of unemployment benefits, you are the quill writer, and the specifics of your job loss are the ink. Record the reasons behind your last employment, whether it was a layoff, resignation, or the end of a brief contract.

Creative Tip: Put yourself in the shoes of a medieval scribe, meticulously recording the ups and downs of your career. Your thorough record acts as the narrative's ink, guiding you through the maze of unemployment.

Details of Bank Accounts

To navigate unexplored areas, a cartographer requires a comprehensive map. Your bank account information is your navigator through the financial terrain when it comes to unemployment benefits. Provide your account details to ensure a seamless transfer of benefits into your treasure chest.

Creative Tip: See the details of your bank account as the map guiding you through the financial assistance landscape. Every number and account detail is a checkpoint ensuring you arrive at a stable destination.

Effective and Creative Success Suggestions

The Treasure Hunter's Compass: Unemployment benefits are the treasure, and even after acquiring them, your search is far from over. Consider extra resources as your compass, leading you to workshops, skill-building courses, and networking opportunities. Keep exploring to uncover treasures that expand your professional toolkit.

Creative Tip: See extra resources as undiscovered gems waiting to be found. Use your treasure hunter's compass to enhance your search, navigating through opportunities to uncover insightful knowledge and abilities.

The Alchemist's Elixir: Approach the curves with the same optimism as the alchemist searching for the key to resilience. View failures as chances to grow and change, transforming obstacles into learning opportunities that advance your career. The optimistic outlook propelling you forward is the alchemist's elixir.

Creative Tip: See yourself as the alchemist transforming the difficulties associated with unemployment into the potent remedy for resilience. Every obstacle serves as a component in the alchemical reaction that fortifies your determination.

Imagine yourself as the hero of an epic story, equipped with the scribe's quill, the cartographer's map, the wizard's grimoire, and the time-travel amulet as you embark on filing for unemployment benefits. Turn employment vacancies into diplomatic talks and eligibility issues into riddles that need solving. Even after receiving unemployment benefits, keep navigating opportunities with the treasure hunter's compass. Retain the alchemist's optimistic outlook and turn obstacles into opportunities. Your pursuit of stability becomes an artistic journey, with every document, obstacle, and accomplishment serving as a brushstroke on the canvas of your career narrative—an exciting adventure just waiting to happen.

Will Applying for Unemployment affect Me

Embarking on the voyage of applying for unemployment benefits is akin to setting sail on a creative odyssey. In the vast sea of uncertainties, concerns about how this quest might influence you can emerge like mermaids beckoning from the depths. Fear not, intrepid reader, for this guide serves as a compass, leading you through the tides and uncovering the creative nuances of how applying for unemployment might alter your professional trajectory.

Financial Stability

Imagine the act of applying for unemployment as a stone flung into the tranquil waters of your financial lake. The ripples that radiate signify the possible impact on your stability. Unemployment benefits operate as a lifebuoy, keeping you afloat during the harsh seas of Unemployment. This temporary support can give a cushion, helping you withstand the stormy waves while sailing toward new work prospects.

Creative Tip: Envision your financial stability as a serene lake. The ripples from applying for unemployment are not disruptions but rather momentary perturbations, affording you a lifeline until the waters clear, and your professional ship sets sail once more.

Rebuilding Professional Confidence

Applying for unemployment may feel like a trek through the ashes, but remember, the phoenix rises from the ashes stronger and more brilliant. The act of seeking assistance is not a sign of defeat but a recognition of the temporary challenges you encounter. As you negotiate the unemployment labyrinth, use this time for self-reflection, skill-building, and mapping the course for your successful return to the professional arena.

Creative Tip: Picture yourself as the phoenix, soaring high

above the ashes of uncertainty. The journey of applying for unemployment becomes the ascension, transforming problems into opportunities to emerge stronger and more resilient than before.

Navigating the Job Search Landscape

Applying for unemployment may briefly divert your emphasis from your old employment to the multicolored scene of the job search. This transition is not a detour but a brilliant mosaic of possibilities. Use this time to explore new pathways, discover hidden abilities, and journey into undiscovered territories of your professional kaleidoscope.

Creative Tip: Envision the job hunt scene as a kaleidoscope, each spin revealing a different dimension of your potential. The path of unemployment becomes a creative experience, allowing you to rediscover and rebuild your professional identity.

Navigating Emotional Challenges

Applying for unemployment could raise emotional storms, yet these storms are part of the symphony of your professional path. Embrace the emotional crescendos as natural elements, enabling yourself to experience the whole gamut of feelings. Each storm is followed by quiet, and in that peace, you discover the power to continue your creative voyage.

Creative Tip: Imagine your emotions as the notes of a symphony. The trip through unemployment becomes a musical masterpiece, with highs and lows contributing to the emotional complexity of your professional tale.

Finding Hidden Treasures

Unemployment may be a voyage of self-discovery, revealing hidden gems within oneself. As you navigate this mission, you may uncover abilities, skills, or hobbies you never knew existed. Treat each problem as a quest, and amid the labyrinth, you can unearth hidden chambers of self-worth and resilience.

Creative Tip: Picture yourself as the heroic adventurer, finding treasures within the caverns of your being. The journey through unemployment becomes a quest of self-discovery, with each struggle unveiling a hidden gem that adds to the brightness of your professional image.

Practical and Imaginative Tips for Success

Crafting a Narrative for Future Employers

Unemployment is not a blemish on your professional tapestry but a thread in the weaving of your tale. As you apply for unemployment benefits, consider it an opportunity to develop a captivating story for prospective employers. Highlight the abilities you've refined, the hurdles you've faced, and the creative journey you've undertaken throughout this period.

Creative Tip: Envision your professional story as a woven tapestry. The act of applying for unemployment becomes an intentional thread, adding depth and complexity to the meticulous architecture of your narrative.

Navigating a Direction for Future Endeavors

Applying for unemployment might be like consulting a starlit compass to guide your career future. Use this opportunity to set your sights on new goals, dream large, and design a course for future undertakings. The act of obtaining unemployment benefits becomes a heavenly moment, pointing you into new constellations in your career sky.

Creative Tip: Picture your professional trajectory as a starlit sky. The compass of unemployment benefits becomes a tool, helping you navigate among the constellations of opportunities and choose a course for your future professional adventure.

As you set sail on the creative journey of applying for unemployment benefits, consider yourself as the captain of a robust ship, sailing the seas of uncertainty. The ripples, storms, and emotional symphonies are not impediments but aspects of the big narrative of your career path. Embrace the phoenix's ascension, the kaleidoscope of time, and the hidden treasures within. View applying for unemployment not as a setback but as a vital chapter in your epic narrative, contributing to the rich fabric of your career. Remember, dear reader, every storm has a rainbow, and every odyssey, no matter how tough, has the ability to lead to new and colorful shores. May your creative compass guide you through the tides, and may your professional voyage be a narrative of tenacity, self-discovery, and victory.

Chapter 4

Navigating the Application Process

Engaging in the process of filing paperwork is often viewed as a mundane administrative chore, a journey through paperwork mazes navigated with hesitation. What if we could transform this routine task into a creative expedition? An adventure where each step unfolds like strokes on a painting, crafting a masterpiece of clarity and empowerment. In this book, we embark on an innovative trip through the step-by-step process of filing, infusing creativity into each stride to demystify the paperwork maze.

Gather Your Tools

Imagine the process of filing as a call to adventure. Stand at the threshold of paperwork, considering yourself as the hero, armed with a miraculous toolkit. Your tools include identity documents, employment history records, and any other items essential for this mission. Picture these goods as talismans, each possessing a unique power to unlock the doors of bureaucracy.

Creative Tip: Think of your toolkit as a magic bag, each piece within bearing a specific enchantment. The call to adventure becomes an opportunity to wield your magical tools and start on a trip of paperwork exploration.

Navigate to the Online Platform

In the digital age, the portal to paperwork experiences lies within the vast landscapes of internet platforms. Picture the internet platform as a mythical gateway, waiting for you to insert the key. Navigate to the website meant for filing, and when you log in, visualize yourself turning the key that unlocks the portal to a world of administrative possibilities.

Creative Tip: Envision the internet platform as a secret door in a magical forest. As you enter, picture turning a key, unlocking the hidden world where the paperwork adventure unfolds.

Fill in the Blanks

Your next phase in this paperwork journey is the search for information. Picture the forms as ancient scrolls, each blank spot awaiting the quill of your responses. Approach each question with the inventiveness of a storyteller, weaving the tale of your personal and professional path into the blanks. Envision the information as ink, changing the blank canvas of documentation into a tapestry of your unique tale.

Creative Tip: Think of each form as a chapter in your epic narrative. Fill in the blanks with the flair of a storyteller, turning the paperwork into a painting with the brilliant colors of your experiences.

Verify and Review

As you go through the paperwork process, the next stage is to verify and review. Picture this process as an alchemist refining their concoction. Each piece of information you verify is an ingredient, contributing to the wonderful brew of your documentation. Envision yourself as the alchemist, ensuring that the concoction is immaculate, free from faults and ready for submission.

Creative Tip: Think of the verification process as swirling a pot of magical brew. Each detail you verify is a magical component, contributing to the perfection of your paperwork potion.

Turning Hurdles into Quests

Overcome Challenges

Challenges in paperwork might be envisioned as a dance of puzzles. Embrace each problem as a dance step, converting potential stumbling blocks into beautiful moves. Approach hurdles with the inventiveness of a puzzle solver, changing the paperwork dance into a choreography of triumph.

Creative Tip: Picture challenges as dance moves in a dynamic routine. With each stage, envision yourself conquering difficulties, turning the paperwork dance into an art form.

Seek Assistance

Should you find uncharted places in the paperwork arena, consider yourself as a trailblazer seeking instruction from enlightened explorers. Seek assistance via online resources, customer support, or community forums. Picture these exchanges like unearthing ancient maps, guiding you through the unknown landscapes of paperwork.

Creative Tip: Think of getting assistance as beginning an excursion. Your guides, whether online forums or customer service, are like seasoned explorers, offering insights and navigating you through the unexplored paperwork zones.

Learn from Setbacks

Setbacks are not the end but the potential for a phoenix's resurrection. Picture setbacks as a transformative journey, where the problems you experience become the ashes from which you emerge stronger. Envision yourself as the phoenix, soaring over the setbacks, with each challenge adding to the wings of your own resilience.

Creative Tip: Think of setbacks as the phoenix's ascension. Each struggle becomes a transformational flame, motivating you to rise from the ashes and continue your arduous adventure with newfound power.

Practical and Imaginative Tips for Success

Explore Additional Resources

Your paperwork odyssey doesn't finish once the forms are filed. Imagine this phase as a treasure hunt, finding extra resources that can expand your comprehension of the paperwork landscape. Online courses, forums, and expert assistance become secret jewels, waiting to be discovered and integrated into your paperwork repertoire.

Creative Tip: Envision more resources as hidden gems in the paperwork realm. Your exploration becomes a treasure hunt, uncovering jewels of wisdom to enrich your future paperwork adventures.

Plan for the Future

Picture your paperwork trip as a voyage, and now, it's time to plan for the future. Your paperwork and records become the navigator's compass, leading you toward future initiatives. Envision yourself as the captain, charting a course for success with the compass of your paperwork preparedness.

Creative Tip: Think of your documentation as the map for future travels. The navigator's compass guarantees you are well-prepared for the challenges and successes that await you on your professional seas.

As you unfurl the canvas of papers, see each step as a stroke, producing a masterpiece of clarity and empowerment. Transform the commonplace into the spectacular, turning paperwork into a creative voyage. You, the hero of this adventure, use the tools, turn keys, fill scrolls, and brew potions to conquer the paperwork realm.

Embrace hurdles as dancing steps, setbacks as opportunities for transformation, and seek counsel from knowledgeable explorers when the terrain gets tough. Your paperwork journey is not just a set of steps; it's an art form, a creative manifestation of your unique narrative and tenacity.

May your paperwork odyssey be filled with the colors of imagination, the triumphs of problem-solving, and the joy of a masterpiece well-crafted. Safe travels, intrepid traveler, as you traverse the oceans of paperwork with the flair of an artist and the knowledge of a seasoned explorer.

Online vs. In-Person Application

In the captivating realm of job applications, a formidable showdown unfolds – a clash between the virtual warriors of online applications and the valiant heroes of in-person submissions. As job seekers don their metaphorical armor, a pivotal question lingers: Which path shall one choose? Within the pages of this epic narrative, we unravel the intricate fabric of the Online vs. In-Person Application saga, offering you a vivid exploration of the strengths, weaknesses, and subtle nuances that may tip the scales in this employment duel.

Online Applications

Envision online applications as a mystical realm, where job seekers wield digital wands to cast spells on potential employers. In this domain, convenience is the elixir, allowing applicants to summon their professional profiles with a simple click. Picture yourself as the sorcerer, crafting a digital scroll that traverses the ether, conveying your qualifications to the portals of opportunity.

Creative Tip: Visualize the online application procedure as a fantastic journey. Each click is a magical spell, transforming your qualifications into a digital scroll that weaves its way across the enchanting land of the internet, reaching the castles of potential employers.

In-Person Applications

In-person applications, on the other hand, evoke the imagery of a grand parade. Picture yourself as the parade master, confidently marching to the rhythm of your own professional drum. Your résumé is a majestic banner, and your clothes make a statement about your professional regalia. With in-person applications, you traverse the streets of opportunity, leaving a trail of personal impressions in your wake.

Creative Tip: Envision in-person applications as a magnificent procession. Your résumé is the flag guiding the way, and your outfit is the regal attire of a professional warrior. With each stride, you leave behind a trail of personal impressions, marking the streets of opportunity.

Advantages of Online Applications

Online apps are the sorcerer's chosen spell, creating magic with various advantages. The convenience of applying from the comfort of your castle, the ability to cast a wide net across various opportunities, and the quick communication of your professional essence make online applications a formidable force in the job-seeking sphere.

Creative Tip: Picture internet apps as a wonderful potion. The convenience of brewing it in the comfort of your own castle, the wide-reaching impacts as it spreads its enchantment over several possibilities, and the rapid delivery of your professional essence contribute to the potency of this digital concoction.

Disadvantages of Online Applications

Online apps, for all their digital magic, hold flaws reminiscent of navigating an enchanted maze. The possibility for resumes to get lost in the digital ether, the challenge of standing out in a vast pool of applicants, and the impersonal nature of the process may leave job seekers feeling like lost adventurers in the labyrinth.

Creative Tip: Picture internet programs as a magical maze. The propensity for resumes to wander lost in the digital ether, the challenge of sticking out in a maze of applications, and the impersonal nature of the process give a sense of wandering through a magical labyrinth.

Advantages of In-Person Applications

In-person applications, akin to a grand parade, carry strengths that resonate with the nobility of personal connection. The opportunity to make a lasting impression through eye contact, a firm handshake, and the chance to exhibit not just your professional prowess but also your character and charisma adds a regal touch to this approach.

Creative Tip: Envision in-person applications as a royal courtship. Your eye contact and strong handshake become the chivalrous actions of a knight, while the opportunity to demonstrate your character and charisma adds a regal touch to this noble courting.

Disadvantages of In-Person Applications

In-person applications, despite their regal atmosphere, encounter problems reminiscent of a crowded battlefield. The need to allocate time and resources, the potential for limited reach compared to the vastness of the online world, and the need to perform admirably in face-to-face encounters may feel like navigating through the chaotic terrains of a battlefield.

Creative Tip: Envision in-person applications as a crowded battlefield. The necessity to allocate time and resources, the potential for restricted reach, and the need to perform admirably in face-to-face encounters generate a sense of navigating through the stormy terrains of a professional battlefield.

Practical Tips for Success

Balancing Online and In-Person Approaches

The secret to success lies in crafting a smooth tango between online and in-person applications. Picture yourself as a skillful dancer, gliding fluidly between the digital and physical dance floors. Harness the strengths of both methods, using online applications to cast a wide net and in-person engagements to leave a lasting, personal impression.

Creative Tip: Envision the job-seeking quest as a lovely dance. Glide fluidly between the digital and physical environments, harnessing the strengths of each method. Picture yourself as a skillful dancer orchestrating a harmonic waltz amid the varied landscapes of work options.

Crafting a Consistent Narrative

In your pursuit of employment, consider yourself as a tapestry weaver, constructing a consistent story throughout both online and in-person conversations. Your CV, cover letters, and digital presence become threads in the tapestry of your professional tale. Weave a narrative that easily flows between the virtual and physical environments, delivering a unified and captivating account to potential employers.

Creative Tip: Think of your career narrative as a woven tapestry. Your online and in-person encounters become threads, smoothly mixing to form a cohesive and fascinating story. Envision yourself as a skillful weaver, constructing a tapestry that captivates potential employers.

The struggle between Online and In-Person Applications is not a battle to be won but a strategic dance to be mastered. Envision yourself as the orchestrator of this employment symphony, blending the strengths of each method and navigating the shortcomings with originality and elegance.

Picture online applications as digital spells, casting a wide net across chances, and in-person engagements as a magnificent procession, leaving a trail of personal impressions. Harmonize the abilities, build a cohesive story, and waltz effortlessly through the different landscapes of job seeking.

In the end, it's not about selecting sides but about perfecting the art of both. So, dear job seeker, may your dance be graceful, your tale fascinating, and your trip a symphony of achievement in the big arena of employment.

Chapter 5

Organizing Your Paperwork

*Eight Tips for Organizing
Your Paperwork*

Amidst the intricate dance of daily life, paperwork often assumes the role of a wayward partner, twirling out of control and leaving us bewildered. Fear not, for this guide is your choreographer, presenting a series of user-friendly instructions to transform the chaotic dance into a graceful waltz. Envision yourself as the conductor of an orderly symphony, each document playing its note seamlessly. Embark on the adventure of mastering the art of order and transforming your paperwork from a cacophony into a melodious tune.

Establish a Command Center

Imagine your desk as the stage for the major act of managing your files. Designate a single spot as your command center, a space where the overture of organization begins. Envision yourself as the conductor, orchestrating the parts of your paperwork symphony from this central stage.

Practical Tip: Choose a well-lit and comfortable place for your command center. Ensure it has appropriate storage, like shelves or filing cabinets, to accommodate the many instruments of your paperwork ensemble.

Create Clear Sections

Categorization is the sonata that adds harmony to the paperwork symphony. Visualize your documents as musical notes, each belonging to a specific area in your symphony. Envision yourself as the composer, creating clear categories like "Financial," "Personal," and "Work-related" to organize the many movements of your papers.

Practical Tip: Use labeled folders or color-coded binders to create different categories. This will make it easy to identify specific documents and maintain the harmony of your documentation ensemble.

Establish Naming Conventions

Naming standards are the minuet, a constant dance that ensures each document plays its part perfectly. Picture yourself as the choreographer, providing clear and consistent naming rules for your files. Whether it's by date, project, or type, the goal is to preserve uniformity in nomenclature to maintain the smooth flow of your paperwork dance.

Practical Tip: Develop a simple and intuitive naming system for your documents. For example, use "YYYY-MM-DD_Description" for dated papers or "ProjectName_DocumentType" for project-related files.

Schedule Periodic Check-ins

Regular maintenance is the rondo, a repeating rhythm that keeps your paperwork symphony in tune. Picture yourself as the conductor, arranging periodic check-ins to evaluate and tidy your documents. Envision these check-ins as occasions when you fine-tune the notes of your paperwork ensemble, ensuring everything remains structured and harmonic.

Practical Tip: Set aside dedicated time each month for a paperwork check-in. Use this time to evaluate, eliminate superfluous documents, and ensure that everything is in its appropriate spot.

Break Down Tasks

In the midst of overwhelming paperwork, envision yourself as the composer breaking down a complex symphony into manageable movements. Instead of handling everything at once, focus on one aspect or category at a time. Envision yourself directing a slow crescendo, bringing order to the chaos one note at a time.

Practical Tip: Break down your organizing efforts into smaller, more manageable chunks. For example, allocate one day to arranging financial paperwork and another to organizing personal files.

Set Short-Term Goals

Procrastination is the staccato, the abrupt disruption in the seamless flow of your paperwork symphony. Picture yourself as the conductor setting short-term goals to offset this staccato. Envision these goals as staccato notes, punctuating the beat of your duties and keeping the paperwork ensemble moving forward.

Practical Tip: Set precise and achievable short-term goals for each organizing session. For instance, try to organize a specific folder or category within a set timeframe.

Embrace Technology

Embrace technology as the harmony that elevates your paperwork symphony. Imagine yourself as the technophile conductor, employing scanners, document management software, and cloud storage to digitize and organize your records. Envision the seamless integration of technology as the harmonious blend that enriches the music of your paperwork ensemble.

Practical Tip: Invest in a reliable scanner to digitize tangible documents. Use online storage solutions like Google Drive or Dropbox to establish a digital backup of your documentation, making it instantly accessible and eliminating physical clutter.

Stay Present in the Process

Mindfulness is the ultimate finale, the conclusion of your efforts in mastering the art of order. Picture yourself as the mindful conductor, staying present in the process of arranging your files. Envision the conclusion as the time when you enjoy the harmony you've created, honoring the labor and devotion involved in turning chaos into order.

Practical Tip: Practice awareness during your organizing sessions. Stay focused on the task at hand, enjoy the progress you make, and celebrate the small successes in your paperwork symphony.

As you embark on the journey of organizing your papers, consider yourself as the director of a symphony, each document playing its part in the beautiful music of order. Establish a command center, create clear categories, and implement consistent naming rules to assemble a masterpiece of organization. Schedule occasional check-ins to maintain harmony, break down overwhelming tasks, and set short-term goals to counteract procrastination.

Embrace technology as the harmonious blend that enhances your paperwork symphony, and stay present in the process, relishing the grand conclusion of mindfulness. May your paperwork dance be a graceful waltz, a ballet of order and harmony amid the grand symphony of your working life. Safe travels, conductor of order, as you lead your paperwork orchestra to a crescendo of organizational glory.

Chapter 6

Seven Tips for a Successful Application

In the realm of approvals, be it for loans, credit cards, or various applications, navigating the terrain can often feel like a challenging adventure. Fear not, for this guide serves as your compass, offering user-friendly recommendations not only to navigate but to significantly enhance your odds of approval. Envision yourself as the explorer, armed with the knowledge and methods to unlock the gates to both financial and personal success. Let's embark on this journey of approval mastery, transforming the desire for approval into a triumphant experience.

Know Your Credit Score and Report

Consider your credit score and report as a treasure map, guiding you through the approval landscape. Picture yourself as the explorer, delving into the intricacies of your credit history to grasp your standing. Your credit score acts as the map's key, revealing potential treasures or pitfalls on your adventure.

Practical Tip: Regularly check your credit score and scrutinize your credit record. Rectify any inaccuracies and comprehend the factors influencing your score. This ensures you are well-prepared to navigate the approval landscape.

Maintain a Healthy Debt-to-Income Ratio

Your debt-to-income ratio serves as the potion, a magical elixir capable of altering your approval prospects. Envision yourself as the alchemist, carefully concocting the potion of smart debt management. Aim to maintain a healthy balance, ensuring your income surpasses your debts, portraying yourself to lenders as a stable and low-risk borrower.

Practical Tip: Calculate your debt-to-income ratio by dividing your total monthly debt payments by your gross monthly income. Strive to keep this ratio below 36% to maximize your approval odds.

Build a Strong Financial Reservoir

Your savings act as the shield, providing protection against unexpected hurdles on your approval journey. Envision yourself as the protector, brandishing this shield to signify financial stability. Visualize a substantial savings account as a barrier not only guarding you against financial storms but also boosting your credibility in the eyes of lenders.

Practical Tip: Establish an emergency fund with at least three to six months' worth of living expenses. This financial shield will not only solidify your financial security but also increase your odds of approval.

Research and Compare Lenders

Researching and comparing lenders serve as your knowledge compass, directing you to the most favorable approval destinations. Picture yourself as the navigator, using this compass to explore different lenders, their terms, and approval requirements. Envision an informed journey where each step is guided by your knowledge compass.

Practical Tip: Research and compare lenders before applying for loans or credit cards. Consider interest rates, fees, and approval criteria. This knowledge will empower you to choose lenders aligned with your financial goals and enhance your approval odds.

Addressing Credit Challenges

Credit issues may seem like unbridgeable gaps, but with the bridge builder's toolkit, you become the architect of your financial future. Picture yourself as the builder, using tools like secured credit cards, credit counseling, and prudent financial practices to construct bridges over credit issues. Transform problems into opportunities for improving and strengthening your credit.

Practical Tip: If you have credit issues, utilize secured credit cards to gradually repair your credit. Seek guidance from credit counseling agencies for specialized advice on managing and enhancing your credit.

Communicate with Lenders

Communication with lenders is the negotiator's diplomacy, turning potential rejections into open discussions. Picture yourself as the diplomat, reaching out to lenders when faced with obstacles. Envision a diplomatic interaction where you explain your situation, present new information, and negotiate terms to boost your approval odds.

Practical Tip: If you anticipate issues with your application, proactively reach out to the lender. Communicate relevant information that can strengthen your case and demonstrate your commitment to responsible financial behavior.

Develop a Strategic Approval Plan

Your strategic approval plan is the planner's blueprint, a roadmap guiding you through the twists and turns of the approval process. Picture yourself as the architect, crafting a detailed strategy that includes timelines, financial targets, and specific steps to maximize your approval odds. Envision a well-crafted blueprint translating your dreams into tangible achievements.

Practical Tip: Outline your financial targets, dates, and action steps in a strategic approval plan. This plan will serve as your guide, keeping you focused on the path to success and increasing your approval odds.

As you embark on the journey of maximizing your approval probabilities, see yourself as the intrepid adventurer equipped with the knowledge and methods to tackle hurdles. Your credit score is the treasure map, debt management the potion, savings the shield, and knowledge the compass that guides you. Transform problems into opportunities, communicate effectively, and establish a strategic plan to blueprint your success.

May your approval journey be a triumphant experience, where setbacks become stepping stones, and challenges morph into possibilities. Safe travels, intrepid traveler, as you traverse the landscape of approvals with confidence, resilience, and the keys to unlock the gates to financial and personal achievement.

Chapter 7

Seven Ways to Avoid Unemployment Benefits Claims Common Mistakes

In the intricate web of life's challenges, steering clear of common pitfalls is akin to navigating serene waters with precision. Fear not, for this guide is your reliable compass, offering user-friendly counsel to help you sidestep traps and transform your journey into one of triumph. Picture yourself as the astute navigator, armed with insights and strategies to gracefully navigate the most common difficulties. Let's embark on this journey of error-free navigation, turning potential missteps into opportunities for growth and success.

Clearly Define Your Goals

Visualize your aspirations as unexplored territories waiting to be mapped. See yourself as the meticulous cartographer, methodically outlining the boundaries and landmarks of your ambitions. Avoid the common mistake of vague or ambiguous goals by being Specific, Measurable, Achievable, Relevant, and Time-bound (SMART). Clear goals act as your navigational cues, ensuring you stay on course.

Practical Tip: Document your goals with specificity. Instead of a vague "lose weight," aim for "lose 10 pounds in three months by adopting a healthier diet and exercising three times a week." This precision becomes your map for success.

Avoid Hasty Decision-Making

Hasty decisions are the rough edges that can mar the sculpture of your growth. Envision yourself as the sculptor, carefully chiseling away at the stone of your choices with patience and precision. Steer clear of the common mistake of impulsive decision-making by taking the time to gather information, evaluate alternatives, and analyze implications. Patience is the chisel that transforms decisions into masterpieces.

Practical Tip: Establish a decision-making process that involves gathering information, weighing pros and cons, and taking a moment for reflection before reaching a conclusion. Patience in decision-making is the sculptor's tool for refining your path.

Research Thoroughly

In the landscape of decisions, diligent study is the detective's probe. Picture yourself as the investigator, scrutinizing every clue and delving into the details before drawing conclusions. Avoid the common pitfall of insufficient research by thoroughly examining the nuances of your options. Comprehensive research acts as your magnifying glass, revealing hidden characteristics and ensuring well-informed decision-making.

Practical Tip: Allocate dedicated time for research before making significant decisions. Rely on credible sources, consult experts, and gather as much information as possible. Thorough research is the detective's key to avoiding common traps.

Develop a Strategic Plan

Envision your journey as a construction project, and your strategic plan as the architect's blueprint. See yourself as the architect, crafting a detailed plan that defines your objectives, timelines, and action steps. Avoid the common mistake of traveling without a strategy by constructing a strategic roadmap. Your strategic plan becomes the blueprint guiding you past potential difficulties and ensuring an organized approach to your goals.

Practical Tip: Outline both short-term and long-term goals, along with the specific steps needed to achieve them. Regularly review and adjust your strategic plan to accommodate changes and new insights. The architect's blueprint is your insurance against wandering aimlessly.

Embrace Change

Change is the alchemist's potion, an elixir that transforms misfortune into opportunity. Envision yourself as the alchemist, responding to new situations with grace and adaptability. Avoid the common mistake of resisting change by embracing it as a necessary part of your journey. Adaptability is the alchemist's secret to turning problems into stepping stones.

Practical Tip: Cultivate an attitude of adaptation by viewing change as a natural aspect of life. Embrace new challenges as opportunities for personal and professional growth. The alchemist's versatility is the key to navigating the ever-evolving terrain.

Regularly Assess Your Progress

Regular reflection is the journalist's method of reviewing and polishing your story. Envision yourself as the journalist, periodically reviewing your progress, identifying patterns, and making necessary adjustments. Avoid the common mistake of neglecting to reflect on your path by incorporating regular check-ins into your routine. Reflection is the journalist's lens that provides clarity to your journey.

Practical Tip: Set aside time regularly, whether weekly or monthly, to reflect on your goals, choices, and progress. Keep a journal to capture your discoveries, struggles, and triumphs. The journalist's reflection is your compass for staying on course.

Allow Time for Growth

Growth is the weaver's tapestry, a masterpiece that reveals itself gradually. Picture yourself as the patient weaver, allowing time for your path and successes to mature. Avoid the common mistake of impatience by recognizing that success is a process, not an event. Patience is the weaver's thread that forms a beautiful tapestry over time.

Practical Tip: Set realistic timelines for your goals and understand that true progress takes time. Celebrate small victories along the way and appreciate the journey as much as the destination. The weaver's patience ensures the development of a robust and detailed tapestry.

As you navigate the waterways of life, see yourself as the savvy navigator, armed with the information and methods to avoid common blunders. Clearly define your goals, craft your decisions with patience, research thoroughly, and establish a strategic plan as your blueprint. Transform setbacks into opportunities for growth, welcome change with adaptation, and continually examine your progress through introspection.

May your path be free of common hazards, and may you navigate smooth seas with confidence, resilience, and the wisdom gained from avoiding missteps. Safe travels, intrepid navigator, as you turn potential missteps into possibilities for a triumphant journey.

Chapter 8

Eight Types of Unemployment Benefits Available

This approachable guide aims to demystify the intricacies of accessible benefits, offering insights into the safety nets that enhance various facets of our lives. Envision yourself as the intrepid explorer, navigating through the diverse terrain of benefits to uncover hidden treasures that can contribute to your overall well-being. Let's embark on this adventure of unraveling the tapestry and discovering the myriad benefits that can enrich our lives.

The Safety Net of Healthcare Benefits

Healthcare benefits stand as the safety net guarding against the uncertainties of disease and medical bills. Picture yourself as the vigilant guardian, shielded by the extensive coverage that healthcare benefits provide. These benefits often encompass health insurance, dental coverage, and vision plans, ensuring you can access medical treatment without compromising your financial stability.

Practical Tip: Grasp the specifics of your healthcare benefits, including coverage restrictions, network providers, and any preventative care treatments offered. Regularly assess your strategy to ensure it aligns with your health needs.

The Umbrella of Insurance Benefits

Insurance benefits act as the protective umbrella shielding you from financial storms. Envision yourself as the well-prepared traveler, confident that insurance benefits will offer financial security in times of need. Types of insurance benefits include life insurance, disability insurance, and property insurance. Each acts as a crucial layer of defense against unforeseen circumstances.

Practical Tip: Evaluate your insurance needs based on your lifestyle and circumstances. Adjust coverage as needed, and be aware of policy terms such as coverage limits, deductibles, and exclusions.

Retirement and Savings Plans

Retirement and savings programs serve as the cornerstones sustaining your financial well-being in the long run. Envision yourself as the architect, laying a solid foundation for your future. Employer-sponsored retirement plans, such as 401(k)s, and individual retirement accounts (IRAs), are examples of benefits empowering you to save for the golden years.

Practical Tip: Capitalize on employer-sponsored retirement programs and consistently contribute to your savings accounts. Understand basics like employer matching contributions and explore additional options like Roth IRAs for tax advantages.

The Blanket of Paid Time Off and Leave Benefits

Paid time off and leave benefits act as the comforting blanket allowing you to relax and address personal matters without compromising income. Picture yourself as the well-rested and rejuvenated traveler, enveloped in the comfort of paid leave benefits. These benefits may include vacation days, sick leave, and parental leave.

Practical Tip: Familiarize yourself with your employer's policy on paid time off and leave. Plan and communicate your time-off needs in advance, ensuring a balance between work and personal well-being.

Cafeteria Plans

Cafeteria plans offer a toolkit of customizable benefits, enabling you to build your benefits package tailored to your individual needs. Envision yourself as the artisan, selecting benefits like health savings accounts (HSAs), flexible spending accounts (FSAs), and dependent care support programs. These tools allow you to address specific financial challenges with tax advantages.

Practical Tip: Understand the options available in your employer's cafeteria plan and choose perks that align with your financial goals. Maximize contributions to accounts like HSAs and FSAs for maximum tax benefits.

The Lighthouse of Employee Assistance Programs (EAPs)

Employee Assistance Programs (EAPs) serve as the lighthouse guiding you through personal issues and professional hurdles. Picture yourself as the sailor, navigating with the support of counseling services, mental health resources, and work-life balance aid provided by EAPs. These benefits contribute to a healthy and supportive work environment.

Practical Tip: Familiarize yourself with the services offered by your employer's EAP. Utilize counseling services, training, and tools to efficiently address personal and professional challenges.

Cultivate Career Development Benefits

Career development benefits are the seeds that can sprout into professional advancement. Envision yourself as the gardener, nurturing your skills and ambitions through benefits like tuition reimbursement, training programs, and mentorship opportunities. These benefits foster ongoing learning and skill growth.

Practical Tip: Explore professional development benefits provided by your employer. Take advantage of training programs, pursue higher education with tuition reimbursement, and seek mentorship to promote your professional progress.

Volunteer and Wellness Programs

Volunteer and wellness programs act as the community bridge connecting you to a sense of purpose and overall well-being. Picture yourself as the community builder, engaging in efforts that contribute to both personal and societal wellness. These rewards may include volunteer time off (VTO), wellness challenges, and community participation opportunities.

Practical Tip: Participate in volunteer and wellness programs to cultivate a sense of community and contribute to your overall well-being. Engage in challenges, activities, or initiatives that align with your values and interests.

As you traverse the tapestry of available benefits, consider yourself as the master weaver, constructing a personalized and comprehensive support system. Healthcare benefits shield you from medical uncertainties, insurance benefits act as financial umbrellas, and retirement and savings plans provide a robust foundation for the future. Paid time off and leave benefits offer the comfort of relaxation, cafeteria plans provide flexible tools, and employee assistance programs guide you through personal and professional obstacles.

Customize your benefits tapestry by exploring career growth options and participating in community initiatives. May your path be illuminated by the numerous benefits available, creating a tapestry of support, stability, and personal fulfillment. Safe travels, knowledgeable navigator, as you unravel the tapestry of benefits and establish a strong and well-supported path through life.

Duration and Amount Considerations

In the intricate dance of financial decisions, understanding the nuances of duration and amount is akin to navigating the ebbs and flows of economic seas. This reader-friendly guide seeks to simplify the complexities, providing insights into how the length and magnitude of financial commitments can impact your overall financial well-being. Envision yourself as the seasoned navigator, equipped with the wisdom to steer your financial ship through different currents. Let's embark on this journey of deciphering the intricacies of duration and amount concerns for a smoother financial voyage.

The Time Horizon: Understanding Duration

Duration, in financial terms, refers to the timeframe over which a financial commitment or investment extends. Picture yourself as the time traveler, traversing through the past, present, and future of your financial decisions. Whether it's a loan, investment, or savings goal, understanding the time horizon is vital. Short-term commitments may include credit card payments, while long-term commitments could comprise a mortgage or retirement savings plan.

Practical Tip: Tailor your financial decisions based on the time horizon. Short-term obligations may require more immediate attention and liquidity, while long-term commitments can benefit from strategic planning and patience.

The Currency of Value: Navigating Amount Considerations

Amount concerns encompass the monetary worth associated with financial obligations, investments, or aspirations. Envision yourself as the currency trader, evaluating the worth and influence of numerous financial actions. Whether it's the amount of a loan, the size of an investment, or the target savings goal, understanding the currency of value is vital. Different financial responsibilities come with varying amounts, and understanding their impact on your overall financial picture is vital.

Practical Tip: Conduct a detailed assessment of the amount involved in your financial commitments. Consider how these numbers correspond with your overall financial goals, budget, and risk tolerance. Prioritize high-impact financial decisions and distribute resources accordingly.

Navigating Challenges: Balancing Duration and Amount

The Sail Adjuster's Toolkit: Tailoring Financial Commitments

Tailoring financial obligations includes modifying the sails based on the prevailing winds of your financial condition. Envision yourself as the sail adjuster, ready to change the duration and amount of your obligations to navigate changing situations. This toolkit includes refinancing debts, renegotiating conditions, or altering savings targets to ensure congruence with your current financial picture.

Practical Tip: Regularly assess your financial obligations and goals. If circumstances change, be proactive in altering the period and amount to better suit your financial condition. This sail adjuster's toolkit is your key to retaining financial flexibility.

The Risk Manager's Compass: Assessing Duration and Amount Risks

Assessing the risks connected with length and amount concerns is the compass that guides you through unclear financial waters. Picture yourself as the risk manager, considering potential hazards and obstacles connected to the duration and quantity of your financial decisions. Risks may include interest rate fluctuations, market volatility, or unforeseen expenses that can impair the fulfillment of your financial commitments.

Practical Tip: Before committing to a financial decision, undertake a comprehensive risk assessment. Consider aspects such as interest rate changes, market conditions, and any unforeseen expenses. This risk manager's compass will help you navigate with prudence and forethought.

Practical and Imaginative Tips for Success

The Budget Architect's Blueprint: Integrating Duration and Amount

Your budget serves as the architect's blueprint, merging the factors of time and amount into a unified financial strategy. Envision yourself as the budget architect, carefully constructing a strategy that allocates resources depending on the time frame and monetary value of your commitments. A well-structured budget guarantees that you're not just meeting short-term responsibilities but also making progress toward long-term financial goals.

Practical Tip: Develop a precise budget that covers your income, expenses, and financial goals. Allocate resources according to the length and amount considerations of various obligations. Regularly examine and adapt your budget to reflect changes in your financial landscape.

The Investment Maestro's Symphony: Harmonizing Duration and Amount in Investments

Investments can be likened to a symphony, where the duration and amount of each instrument add to the overall tune. Envision yourself as the investment maestro, harmonizing the duration and amount of your investments to build a balanced and varied portfolio. Short-term investments may include liquid assets like savings accounts, while long-term investments could comprise retirement funds or real estate.

Practical Tip: Diversify your investment portfolio by considering alternative periods and amounts. Short-term investments may give liquidity, while long-term investments offer the possibility for growth. Regularly adjust your portfolio to preserve harmony and alignment with your financial goals.

As you navigate the waves of financial decisions, see yourself as the seasoned navigator, balancing the factors of duration and amount. Understand the time horizon associated with your obligations and analyze the monetary worth attached to various financial decisions. Tailor your obligations using the sail adjuster's toolset, assess hazards with the compass of a risk manager, and incorporate these considerations into a well-structured budget.

Harmonize the time and amount of your investments like a maestro building a symphony. May your financial voyage be smooth and successful, navigating the currents with prudence, adaptability, and a clear knowledge of the duration and amount concerns that create your financial landscape. Safe travels, knowledgeable navigator, as you plan a course towards financial well-being.

Chapter 9

How To Deal with Unemployment Benefits Claim Denial

In the intricate realm of insurance claims and financial setbacks, encountering a denied claim can feel like hitting a roadblock. But fear not, for this article serves as your roadmap to transforming rejection into resolution. Picture yourself as the resilient explorer, armed with the knowledge and methods to navigate the often-challenging terrain of dealing with a refused claim. Let's embark on this journey of understanding the reasons behind claim denials and exploring practical measures to reverse the decision or find alternative solutions.

Three Common Denial Reasons

Imagine the denial letter as a puzzle, each sentence a piece that uncovers the reasoning for the rejection. Envision yourself as the detective, examining the letter to determine why your claim was refused. Common reasons include insufficient documentation, insurance exclusions, or filing errors. Understanding the initial impact is vital to crafting an appropriate reaction.

Picture yourself as the informed investigator, equipped with the expertise to navigate the complexity of understanding why your claim was refused. Let's continue on this journey of shedding light on the common reasons for claim denial and examining practical measures to prevent these problems in the future.

Insufficient or Inaccurate Information

One of the most prevalent causes for denial is insufficient or faulty paperwork. Envision yourself as the diligent archivist, ensuring that every piece of information you supply is precise, thorough, and aligns with the requirements listed in your insurance policy. Missing or erroneous details might create gaps that lead to claim denial.

Practical Tip: Double-check all documentation before making a claim. Ensure that you give correct and comprehensive information, including pertinent receipts, invoices, and any other supporting documents. Being meticulous in your paperwork decreases the possibility of refusal due to insufficient or erroneous information.

Policy Exclusions and Limitations

Policy exclusions and limitations are like hidden traps that might lead to claim denial. Envision yourself as the policy reader, carefully studying the terms and conditions of your insurance policy to find any exclusions or limits that may apply to your claim. Certain events or circumstances may be explicitly excluded from coverage, leading to denial if they are the cause of your claim.

Practical Tip: Familiarize yourself with the terms and conditions of your insurance policy, paying special attention to any exceptions or limitations. If you have issues, contact your insurance provider for clarification before submitting a claim.

Claims Filed Outside Coverage Period

Claims filed outside the coverage period are a timing issue that might result in denial. Envision yourself as the calendar keeper, ensuring that your claim is filed within the specified term outlined in your policy. Failing to submit your claim during the coverage period can lead to automatic denial, as the insurance provider may not be compelled to honor claims beyond this window.

Practical Tip: Be aware of the coverage term indicated in your policy. Submit your claim well within the prescribed deadline to avoid denial owing to claims filed outside the coverage period. Set reminders or alerts to stay organized with filing deadlines.

Four Strategies to Avoid Common Denial Reasons

Regular Policy Reviews

Regular policy evaluations are the proactive planner's technique to stay aware of any changes in coverage, exclusions, or limitations. Envision yourself as the planner, organizing frequent evaluations of your insurance policy to ensure that you are aware of any revisions or upgrades. Policy changes might affect the coverage of specific events or circumstances, and being informed helps you prevent claim denial due to obsolete policy information.

Practical Tip: Set a calendar reminder to evaluate your insurance coverage at least once a year. Look for any updates, revisions, or amendments that may affect your coverage. Stay proactive in understanding your insurance to avert surprises during the claims process.

Accuracy in Documentation

Accuracy in documentation is the detail-oriented filer's secret to avoiding claim denial. Envision yourself as the careful archivist, paying special attention to every detail when compiling and submitting your claim. Accurate and full documentation not only improves your case but also decreases the possibility of refusal due to missing or inaccurate information.

Practical Tip: Create a checklist of essential papers before submitting a claim. Double-check each item on the list to confirm accuracy and completeness. Attention to detail in your documentation raises the likelihood of a successful claim.

Strategic Communication with Your Provider

Strategic contact with your insurance provider is the claim strategist's strategy to addressing probable denial issues. Envision yourself as the strategist, maintaining open and proactive communication with your insurance company. If you have questions or concerns regarding your coverage or claim, reaching out to your provider for clarification helps prevent misconceptions that may lead to denial.

Practical Tip: Establish a communication channel with your insurance provider. If you are confused about any aspect of your coverage or the claims process, seek clarification before submitting your claim. Proactive communication helps develop a shared understanding and decreases the possibility of denial due to misunderstandings.

Staying Informed About Policy Changes

Staying informed about policy changes is the continuous learner's technique for avoiding claim denial surprises. Envision yourself as the learner, being proactive in seeking knowledge about any revisions or additions to your insurance coverage. Regularly check for messages from your insurance provider, and actively seek information regarding changes in coverage, exclusions, or limitations.

Practical Tip: Subscribe to email notifications or newsletters from your insurance provider to be updated about policy changes. Take the initiative to inquire about any revisions that may affect your coverage. Being a constant learner guarantees that you are always up-to-date with your policy specifics.

As you traverse the complexities of insurance claims, consider yourself as the informed investigator, understanding the reasons for denial and taking proactive actions to prevent traps. Understand the common causes for refusal, be precise in your paperwork, and remain informed about policy changes. Proactively interact with your insurance provider, request clarification when needed, and have a continual learning mindset to keep ahead of potential denial difficulties.

May your future claims be successful, and may you navigate the insurance landscape with confidence, knowledge, and a proactive attitude to ensure a smooth and successful claims process. Safe travels, expert detective, as you decipher the riddles of claim denials and pave the route for financial security.

Five Steps for Appealing a Denied Claim

Before delving into the appeal procedure, envision yourself as the claim detective, deciphering the riddle behind the denial. Carefully analyze the denial letter, stressing the specific grounds for rejection. Common reasons include insufficient documentation, insurance exclusions, or filing errors. Understanding the denial grounds is vital as it lays the foundation for drafting a compelling argument.

Practical Tip: Thoroughly examine the refusal letter and discover the exact reasons for rejection. Cross-reference these explanations with your initial claim and policy documentation to achieve a clear understanding. This clarity will drive your appeal strategy.

Review Your Policy

Envision yourself as the planner, evaluating your insurance policy with a fine-tooth comb. Policy specifics, exclusions, and limitations play a key part in the appeal process. Familiarize yourself with the terms and conditions of your policy, giving special attention to phrases that may relate to the reasons for denial. A comprehensive comprehension of your policy increases your appeal.

Practical Tip: Take time to check your insurance coverage thoroughly. Look for any relevant information connected to the denial reasons. If you have issues or need clarification, reach out to your insurance provider for assistance.

Gather Supporting Evidence

As the documentarian, see yourself compiling a formidable armory of supporting evidence. This material functions as your ammunition during the appeal procedure. Gather any missing or extra paperwork that addresses the reasons for denial. This may include medical documents, receipts, or any other pertinent information that improves your case.

Practical Tip: Create a checklist of required documents depending on the denial reasons. Collect any essential records, ensuring they correspond with the appeal plan. A well-documented case boosts your chances of a successful appeal.

Craft a Compelling Appeal Letter

Now, envision yourself as the appeal architect, drafting a great appeal letter. This is your moment to explain your case persuasively. Address each reason for denial separately, providing more information, context, and documentation. Be brief, clear, and strong in your words, highlighting why your point should be examined.

Practical Tip: Structure your appeal letter in a clear and structured manner. Begin by identifying the denial reasons, followed by a full explanation and supporting evidence for each. Conclude with a forceful and confident plea for the reversal of the denial.

Engage with Your Insurance Provider

Effective communication is the key to success. Envision yourself as the communicator, reaching out to your insurance provider to discuss the denial, seek clarity, and indicate your intent to appeal. Establishing a pleasant and open line of communication can sometimes lead to insights, alternative ideas, or even a resolution without the need for a formal appeal.

Practical Tip: Contact your insurance carrier quickly after receiving the denial notice. Express your readiness to appeal and inquire about any more information or steps you may do to remedy the issues. Maintain a professional and respectful tone in your communications.

Seek Professional Assistance

As the collaborator, see yourself requesting expert aid if needed. Insurance claim adjusters, attorneys, or consumer advocacy organizations specialize in negotiating the complexities of the appeals process. If you find the appeal onerous or complex, consulting with professionals can provide expert guidance and support.

Practical Tip: If you face difficulties or feel overwhelmed by the appeal procedure, consider getting expert guidance. Consult with an insurance claim adjuster, attorney, or consumer advocacy organization to receive expert advice specific to your circumstance.

Practical and Imaginative Tips for Success

Stay Persistent and Patient

Persistence and patience are the trademarks of the optimist. Appeals can take time, and it's crucial to stay diligent in your pursuit. Follow up with your insurance provider often to check on the status of your appeal. Patience is your ally while you traverse the bureaucratic processes and work towards a resolution.

Practical Tip: Establish a timeline for follow-up discussion with your insurance provider. Be diligent in requesting updates on your appeal status while retaining patience throughout the process. A balance of tenacity and patience will serve you well.

Know Your Rights

As the empowered consumer, consider yourself being aware of your rights during the appeals process. Familiarize yourself with the legislation and guidelines that regulate insurance claims in your jurisdiction. Knowing your rights helps you to advocate successfully and guarantees that you are treated fairly throughout the appeal process.

Practical Tip: Research and understand the legislation and consumer rights connected to insurance claims in your location. If you believe your rights are not being honored, don't hesitate to bring it to the attention of your insurance provider or relevant regulatory authorities.

As you engage on the path of appealing a denied claim, see yourself as the dedicated advocate, regaining what is properly yours. Understand the denial reasons, evaluate your policy, gather supporting information, and draft a strong appeal letter. Engage with your insurance provider, seek expert aid if needed, and retain tenacity and patience throughout the process.

May your appeal be successful, leading to a conclusion that aligns with your requirements and financial well-being. Safe travels, determined advocate, as you navigate the appeals process and transform setbacks into opportunities for financial recovery.

Chapter 10

Eight Powerful Unemployment Interview Strategies

Navigating the unemployment interview process can pose challenges, but armed with the right strategies, you can transform it into a steppingstone toward your next professional opportunity. Visualize yourself as the interview virtuoso, well-prepared with information and techniques to excel in unemployment interviews. This user-friendly guide aims to provide insights into effective methods, ensuring you make a lasting impression and enhance your chances of securing your next professional chapter.

Know Your State's Unemployment Policies

Before stepping into the interview, envision yourself as the research master, thoroughly understanding the unemployment regulations relevant to your state. Different states may have varying eligibility standards and rules. Being well-informed about your state's policies positions you as a knowledgeable candidate, ready to address inquiries and provide accurate information during the interview.

Practical Tip: Research your state's unemployment regulations and requirements. Familiarize yourself with eligibility rules, benefit levels, and the length of benefits. Being well-informed will boost your confidence and ability to navigate questions linked to your unemployment claim.

Craft a Clear and Honest Narrative

As the storyteller, see yourself weaving a clear and honest tale about your work circumstance. Be prepared to articulate the events that led to your unemployment, emphasizing facts and maintaining transparency. Crafting an engaging yet truthful tale helps create a great impression and demonstrates your communication skills.

Practical Tip: Outline a clear narrative that explains the reasons behind your unemployment. Focus on the facts, stressing any changes in your employment status that were beyond your control. Practice delivering your story to achieve clarity and coherence during the interview.

Showcase Your Job Search Efforts

Envision yourself as the solutions architect, showcasing the efforts you've made in your job search journey. Provide details about the actions you've taken to secure a new job, such as networking, applying to openings, and upskilling. Demonstrating your proactive attitude and commitment to re-entering the workforce will considerably improve your prospects.

Practical Tip: Prepare a record of the activities you've completed in your job hunt, including networking events attended, job applications filed, and skills development projects. Use concrete examples to highlight your dedication to finding a new opportunity.

Frame Your Experience Positively

The positive communicator excels at framing experiences in an upbeat perspective. Visualize yourself focusing on the lessons acquired and abilities obtained during your prior career, rather than dwelling on the circumstances of your departure. Emphasize your resilience and preparedness to contribute effectively to a new work setting.

Practical Tip: Practice framing your past work experience in a positive light. Identify relevant talents, achievements, and lessons learned from your former employment that you can mention during the interview. Projecting a positive attitude can positively influence the interviewer's perception.

Addressing Problems Head-On

The rebuttal specialist excels in addressing problems head-on. Visualize yourself as someone who can confidently reply to potential issues voiced by the interviewer. If there are gaps in your employment history or special circumstances surrounding your unemployment, be prepared to address them proactively, providing context and reassurance.

Practical Tip: Anticipate potential worries or queries connected to your unemployment. Develop clear and succinct comments that address these issues while showcasing your qualifications, talents, and commitment to seeking new job.

Seek Guidance from Employment Agencies

The resourceful navigator seeks help from job agencies and career counselors. Envision yourself reaching out to these specialists for guidance and suggestions on how to navigate unemployment interviews effectively. They can provide valuable advice, offer practice interviews, and help you refine your approach.

Practical Tip: Connect with local job agencies or career counselors who specialize in supporting individuals throughout spells of unemployment. Seek their assistance on interview methods, typical questions, and best practices. Leverage their experience to better your interview preparation.

Fake interviewer

The fake interviewer is your practice buddy, helping you

refine your responses and build confidence. Envision yourself rehearsing frequent interview questions linked to your jobless condition. Solicit input from friends, family, or job mentors to refine your responses and delivery.

Practical Tip: Conduct practice interviews focused on questions pertaining to your unemployment. Practice defining your narrative, addressing problems, and demonstrating your job search efforts. The more you practice, the more comfortable and confident you'll become.

Send a Thank-You Note

The follow-up champion excels at sending insightful thank-you notes following an interview. Envision yourself expressing gratitude for the opportunity to discuss your candidacy and emphasizing your passion for the position. A well-crafted thank-you note exhibits professionalism and makes a great impression.

Practical Tip: Send a thank-you note within 24 hours of your unemployment interview. Express appreciation for the interviewer's time, reiterate your interest in the position, and briefly highlight significant topics that showcase your qualifications. A handwritten thank-you note can set you apart from other contenders.

As you prepare for an unemployment interview, see yourself as the interview virtuoso, well-prepared with excellent tactics to navigate the process successfully. Research your state's unemployment policies, develop a clear and honest narrative, and display your proactive job-seeking activities. Frame your experience favorably, handle concerns proactively, and seek help from job agencies or career counselors.

Practice, seek criticism, and harness the knowledge of specialists to develop your technique. Remember to send a thank-you note as a last touch to create a positive and lasting impression. By mastering the art of unemployment interviews, you portray yourself as a resilient and capable candidate ready for your next career chapter. Safe travels, interview virtuoso, as you embark on this journey of recovering your career path with confidence and conviction.

Unemployment Benefits Claims
Interview Preparation Tips

In the magnificent tapestry of achievement, preparation is the loom that weaves success. Whether you're preparing up for an exam, interview, or a key life event, see yourself as the master of preparation, ready with smart ways to manage hurdles and emerge successful. This user-friendly guide offers practical and inventive preparation strategies to help you not only meet but exceed your goals. Let's go on this road of preparation, where discipline meets creativity, and success becomes an attainable masterpiece.

The Visionary Planner: Set Clear Goals As the visionary planner, see yourself setting clear and achievable goals. Before entering into any endeavor, take a moment to clarify what success looks like. Break down your goals into smaller, attainable chunks, establishing a roadmap that leads your preparation journey. A well-defined vision provides direction, drive, and a sense of accomplishment as you develop.

Practical Tip: Start with a clear vision of your end aim. Break it down into tiny, doable tasks. Whether it's acing a test, excelling in a project, or thriving in an interview, defining clear goals is the first step toward effective preparation.

The Time Management Maestro: Create a Schedule Envision yourself as the time management maestro, organizing your preparation with a well-crafted timetable. Time is an important resource, and using it efficiently is crucial for successful preparation. Create a realistic timeline that allocates devoted time for each component of your preparation, ensuring a balanced and concentrated approach.

Practical Tip: Use tools like calendars, planners, or productivity apps to establish a precise schedule. Prioritize projects depending on their relevance and timeframes. A well-organized timetable guarantees that you cover all parts of your preparation without feeling overwhelmed.

The Resourceful Researcher: Gather Information The resourceful researcher succeeds at acquiring relevant information. Envision yourself delving into the sea of knowledge, acquiring resources, materials, and insights vital for your preparation. Whether it's for an exam, project, or presentation, rigorous research creates the foundation for a well-informed and productive preparation strategy.

Practical Tip: Identify credible sources of knowledge relating to your preparation. Utilize textbooks, online resources, articles, and expert viewpoints. A deep comprehension of the topic matter boosts your confidence and preparation efficiency.

The Practice Prodigy: Embrace Mock Scenarios Embrace your inner practice prodigy by visualizing yourself immersed in fake settings. Whether it's training for an interview, presenting a presentation, or handling exam questions, simulation exercises prepare you for the real deal. Envisioning and rehearsing probable circumstances strengthen your talents, raise confidence, and perfect your approach.

Practical Tip: Create simulated scenarios that mimic the actual circumstance you're prepared for. Practice answering common interview questions, mimic test settings, or rehearse your presentation in front of a mirror or with a trusted friend. The more you practice, the more prepared and confident you'll become.

The Adaptable Navigator: Be Ready for Curveballs As the flexible navigator, see oneself being ready to navigate unanticipated challenges. Life is full of surprises, and preparing means anticipating and reacting to unforeseen occurrences. Whether it's a sudden change in plans or an unexpected question in an interview, maintaining flexibility in your preparation strategy guarantees you can pivot when needed.

Practical Tip: During your preparation, actively introduce changes or challenges to imitate real-life unpredictability's. This could mean tackling a new sort of question, modifying your learning setting, or adapting your presentation to different scenarios. Building adaptability into your preparation routine boosts your resilience.

The Reflective Practitioner: Learn from Mistakes The reflective practitioner sees mistakes as opportunities for improvement. Envision yourself as someone who learns from setbacks rather than getting discouraged by them. Mistakes are an inevitable part of the preparation process, and perceiving them as useful lessons allows you to refine your approach, find areas for development, and evolve as a prepared individual.

Practical Tip: After each practice session or preparation milestone, take time to reflect on what went well and where improvements may be made. Consider mistakes as feedback, change your approach accordingly, and use them as steppingstones toward development.

What to Expect During the Interview

As the first glimpse artist, envision yourself generating a positive impression from the moment you enter the interview location. Your appearance, body language, and early greetings add to the interviewer's first impression. Project confidence, maintain eye contact, and deliver a strong handshake if in-person or a warm hello in a virtual setting.

Practical Tip: Dress appropriately for the corporate culture and the position you're interviewing for. Practice a confident and friendly introduction, ensuring you establish a favorable first impression that lasts.

Answering with Confidence

Envision yourself as the eloquent responder during the Q&A session. Most interviews comprise a sequence of questions aimed to examine your qualifications, talents, and cultural fit. Respond with clarity, provide specific examples, and illustrate how your experiences connect with the needs of the role.

Practical Tip: Practice answering frequent interview questions with a friend or in front of a mirror. Use the STAR approach (Situation, Task, Action, Result) to structure your responses. Be concise, focused, and present your qualifications efficiently.

Handling Curveball Questions

The unexpected twist handler navigates through curveball queries with ease. Interviewers could throw unexpected questions your way to test your ability to think on your feet. Envision yourself staying composed, taking a minute to gather your thoughts, and offering intelligent responses even in the face of unexpected questioning.

Practical Tip: Anticipate potential curveball questions and prepare solutions in advance. If you receive an unexpected inquiry, take a deep breath, ponder your answer, and respond boldly. The capacity to handle the unexpected indicates your versatility and quick thinking.

Dealing with Pauses

As the silence conqueror, envision yourself relishing pauses during the interview. Silence might be uncomfortable, but don't rush to fill it. Take a moment to gather your thoughts before responding. This technique conveys confidence and wisdom.

Practical Tip: Embrace pauses during the interview. If faced with a challenging question, take time to organize your thoughts before responding. It's preferable to deliver a well-thought-out explanation than to rush into a response.

Managing Virtual Interviews

Virtual interviews demand the multitasking maestro to handle technology and conversation concurrently. Envision yourself dominating the virtual interview terrain by securing a stable internet connection, familiarizing yourself with the video platform, and maintaining clear and focused conversation.

Practical Tip: Test your internet connection and familiarize yourself with the video platform before the interview. Ensure you are in a peaceful and well-lit location. Maintain eye contact, dress professionally, and remove distractions to create a polished online appearance.

As you prepare for interviews, see yourself as the intrepid explorer, armed with the abilities to navigate the interview landscape successfully. Thorough preparation, a strong first impression, confident responses, and the capacity to handle unforeseen twists are crucial factors to master. Embrace the challenges, conquer potential impediments, and anticipate success at every stage.

Incorporate practical suggestions such as navigating pauses, mastering virtual interviews, asking insightful questions, and expressing thanks to boost your entire interview experience. Safe travels, intrepid explorer, as you enter the interview environment with confidence, preparedness, and the vision of a prosperous career adventure ahead.

Practical Tips for Success

The Visualization Artist: Envision Success The visualization artist crafts a mental picture of success. Envision yourself attaining your goals and experiencing the happiness that comes with effective planning. Visualization is a strong tool that taps into the mind's potential to influence behaviors. Positive mental imagery boosts motivation, reduces worry, and promotes a conviction in your talents.

Practical Tip: Set aside time for visualization exercises. Close your eyes and vividly visualize yourself effectively navigating the scenarios you're prepared for. Whether it's acing an exam, delivering a spectacular presentation, or excelling in an interview, imagine the process and conclusion with confidence and happiness.

The Mindful Break Taker: Incorporate Rest and Rejuvenation The thoughtful break taker realizes the need of rest in the preparation path. Envision yourself taking breaks thoughtfully, allowing your mind and body to recharge. Overworking can lead to burnout and decreased efficiency. Incorporate short pauses, participate in activities you enjoy, and prioritize appropriate sleep to ensure you approach your preparation with focus and enthusiasm.

Practical Tip: Schedule regular breaks during your preparation sessions. Use these pauses to step away from your job, stretch, take a stroll, or indulge in activities that soothe and replenish you. Mindful breaks aid to general well-being and keep your preparation momentum.

As you go on your road of preparation, see yourself as the master of success, prepared with effective ways to manage hurdles and achieve your goals. Set clear objectives, manage your time carefully, obtain essential knowledge, and embrace the power of practice and adaptation.

Overcome challenges with resilience, learn from failures, and apply visualization techniques into your preparation routine. Remember to take thoughtful breaks, emphasize self-care, and approach your trip with confidence, inventiveness, and a resolve to succeed. Safe travels, preparation master, as you weave your road to success and unlock the doors to a brighter and more accomplished future.

Chapter 11

Taxes and Unemployment Benefits

Embarking on the intersection of taxes and unemployment may seem like a daunting journey, but envision yourself as the savvy navigator, ready to untangle the intricacies and confidently steer through this labyrinth. This user-friendly guide is here to walk you through the essentials, potential challenges, and practical advice, ensuring that tax season becomes a manageable journey, even amid unexpected changes in your employment status.

Tax Implications of Unemployment Benefits

Embarking on the journey of unemployment not only brings financial challenges but also navigates the often-overlooked terrain of tax implications. Envision yourself as the informed explorer, armed with the knowledge to navigate the tax landscape during periods of unemployment. This user-friendly guide aims to illuminate the nuances of tax issues associated with unemployment benefits, offering practical insights and ideas to help you traverse this aspect of your financial journey.

Understanding the Basics

Picture yourself as the taxable income pathfinder, journeying through the fundamental premise that unemployment benefits are considered taxable income. Both at the federal and state levels, a portion of your unemployment compensation is subject to taxation. Similar to your regular income, taxes need to be considered when managing your money during unemployment.

Practical Tip: Allocate a percentage of your unemployment benefits for taxes to minimize unexpected financial strain when tax season begins. Understanding the core concept of taxable income ensures that you are financially prepared for the ramifications of unemployment benefits.

Reporting Unemployment Benefits on Your Tax Return

As the form filer, envision yourself appropriately reporting your unemployment benefits on your tax return. Form 1099-G is the document supplied by the government that reports the entire amount of unemployment benefits received during the tax year. This form is essential for correctly filing your federal and state income taxes.

Practical Tip: Ensure that you obtain Form 1099-G from the entity distributing your unemployment compensation. Keep this form in a safe and immediately accessible place for reference while submitting your taxes. Accurate reporting is vital to prevent errors that could lead to increased tax payments or penalties.

Adjusting Your Tax Withholding

Envision yourself as the withholding wizard, prepared to change your tax withholding to correspond with your present financial circumstances. By default, federal income tax is not withheld from unemployment benefits, but you have the option to request voluntary withholding. Adjusting your withholding helps you manage your tax liability and avert a big tax bill when submitting your annual return.

Practical Tip: Consider asking for voluntary withholding on your unemployment benefits to offset any tax responsibilities. Consult the IRS withholding calculator or seek assistance from a tax professional to determine the right amount to withhold based on your financial situation.

Organizing Your Financial Documents

The record-keeping master envisions themselves maintaining ordered financial records. Accurate paperwork is vital for a seamless tax-filing procedure. Keep careful records of your unemployment benefits, any taxes withheld, and other important financial information to ensure a flawless and stress-free tax season.

Practical Tip: Create a dedicated folder or digital file to store any paperwork connected to your unemployment benefits and taxes. This may include Form 1099-G, verification of any voluntary withholding, and other related financial information. Organizing your documents streamlines the tax preparation procedure.

Overcoming Tax-Time Obstacles

Know Your State's Tax Policies

As the state-specific trailblazer, imagine navigating the unique tax rules of your state. States have varied policies regarding unemployment benefits and taxation. Some may not tax unemployment benefits, while others have differing rules for how benefits are taxed.

Practical Tip: Research and understand your state's specific tax rules related to unemployment compensation. This knowledge ensures compliance with state regulations and prepares you for any state-specific tax ramifications.

Consider Quarterly Payments

Envision yourself as the estimated tax prodigy, contemplating periodic payments if necessary. While federal income tax is typically not deducted from unemployment benefits, you may have the option to make anticipated tax payments during the year. This prevents a substantial tax bill when filing your annual return.

Practical Tip: If anticipating a high tax bill due to unemployment benefits, explore the option of making quarterly anticipated tax payments to the IRS. This approach can help distribute the tax burden and reduce financial strain during tax season.

Leverage Tax Resources

The resourceful seeker sees themselves leveraging available tax resources. Numerous resources, both online and offline, provide essential information and tools to tackle tax-related issues during unemployment. Explore IRS literature, online tax calculators, and seek assistance from tax specialists or financial consultants.

Practical Tip: Familiarize yourself with IRS publications and resources related to unemployment benefits taxation. Utilize online tools and calculators to assess your tax liability and explore potential deductions. Seeking guidance from tax professionals ensures precise and individualized advice.

Plan Ahead for Tax Season

The proactive planner envisions planning ahead for tax season. Instead of viewing taxes as an annual hardship, consider adopting a proactive strategy throughout the year. Regularly assess your financial condition, adjust your withholding as needed, and stay informed about changes in tax regulations that may impact your circumstances.

Practical Tip: Schedule monthly reviews of your financial circumstances, especially with changes in your job status. Stay informed about updates to tax legislation that may affect unemployment benefits. Proactive planning avoids surprises and allows for more effective tax management.

As you navigate the intricate relationship between taxes and unemployment, envision yourself as the astute navigator armed with the tools to make this voyage not only manageable but empowering. Understand the basics, adjust your withholding, maintain accurate records, and explore potential deductions. Be aware of your state's tax policies, consider quarterly payments if necessary, and leverage available resources.

Plan ahead, stay proactive, and view taxes as a navigable landscape rather than an overwhelming challenge. With these practical and inventive recommendations, you can approach tax season with confidence, ensuring that your financial path during periods of unemployment remains as smooth as possible. Safe travels, clever navigator, as you chart your course through the intersection of taxes and unemployment.

Eight Tips for Navigating Taxes Effectively

Embarking on the journey of adulting often introduces us to the perpetual component of life—taxes—an area that can evoke uncertainty and dread. But fear not, for you are about to embark on a path of financial understanding, navigating taxes with confidence. Picture yourself as the financial maestro, armed with practical and user-friendly advice to transform tax season into a comfortable and empowering experience. This tutorial is designed to demystify the intricacies of taxes, offering insights to help you navigate this crucial aspect of personal finance effectively.

Start Early

Imagine yourself as the proactive planner, taking an early initiative in handling your taxes. Waiting until the last minute might lead to tension and potential blunders. Commence organizing your financial paperwork, including income statements, deductions, and credits, well before the tax deadline.

Practical Tip: Set aside a dedicated period each month to evaluate and arrange your financial paperwork. Maintain a separate folder or digital space to store receipts, pay stubs, and any other relevant paperwork. Starting early enables you to identify potential concerns and seek support if needed.

Identify Eligible Deductions

Envision yourself as the deduction detective, seeking out appropriate deductions to maximize your tax savings. Familiarize yourself with popular deductions, such as those for education expenses, medical charges, and charitable contributions. Take advantage of any deductions that pertain to your financial condition.

Practical Tip: Research tax deductions appropriate to your circumstances. Keep comprehensive records of qualified expenses, ensuring you have the necessary evidence to support your deductions. Being a deduction detective can dramatically lower your taxable income.

Maintain Meticulous Records

As the record-keeping virtuoso, imagine yourself maintaining meticulous records throughout the year. Accurate paperwork is vital for a seamless tax-filing procedure. Keep track of income statements, receipts, and other financial data to support your tax return.

Practical Tip: Utilize digital tools like expense tracking apps or spreadsheets to preserve detailed data. Categorize your costs, making it easier to find deductions and credits during tax season. Meticulous record-keeping ensures that you have the relevant information at your fingertips.

Leverage Online Resources

Envision yourself as the tech-savvy taxpayer, utilizing online resources to streamline the tax-filing process. Numerous online tools and software platforms can guide you through the preparation of your tax return, delivering step-by-step guidance and ensuring accuracy.

Practical Tip: Explore trusted tax software or online platforms that align with your needs. Many of these applications feature a user-friendly interface, e-filing choices, and real-time calculations, making the procedure smoother and more accessible.

Stay Informed About Tax Changes

As the knowledge seeker, imagine yourself staying informed about changes to tax rules and regulations. Tax rules might evolve, and being aware of any updates ensures that you are accurately following current guidelines.

Practical Tip: Subscribe to newsletters from reliable financial websites or government tax organizations to stay current on tax-related news. Attend workshops or webinars that provide insights into changes in tax rules. Staying knowledgeable allows you to make informed decisions and navigate tax difficulties efficiently.

Seek Professional Advice

Envision yourself as the collaboration master, recognizing when to seek professional guidance. While internet tools are important, complex financial situations may benefit from the expertise of a tax professional. Consult with a trained tax advisor to ensure that you are optimizing your deductions and credits.

Practical Tip: If you have a complex financial situation, operate a business, or experience significant life changes, seek the assistance of a tax specialist. They can provide specialized guidance, answer specific questions, and guide you through potential obstacles.

Create a Tax Preparation Checklist

The checklist champion envisions oneself establishing a tax preparation checklist to stay organized. Develop a comprehensive checklist that contains all the documents and information required for your tax return. Use this checklist as a roadmap to guarantee that you don't overlook any vital items.

Practical Tip: Customize your checklist based on your financial circumstances. Include categories such as income statements, deductions, credits, and supporting documentation. Having a checklist speeds up the tax preparation process and decreases the danger of overlooking vital information.

Use Tax Refunds Wisely

Imagine yourself as the conscientious budgeter, effectively budgeting for your tax refund. Rather than perceiving your refund as a windfall, consider using it as a tool to boost your financial well-being. Allocate funds toward savings, debt repayment, or investments that align with your long-term financial goals.

Practical Tip: Develop a strategy for your tax refund that corresponds with your financial priorities. Consider creating an emergency fund, paying off high-interest debt, or investing in retirement accounts. Being a diligent budgeter ensures that your tax refund adds to your overall financial success.

As you traverse the world of taxes, envision yourself as the financial maestro, mastering the art of tax preparation with confidence and foresight. Start early, discover qualified deductions, maintain thorough records, and harness online tools. Stay educated about tax developments, get professional counsel when needed, and create a tax preparation checklist for organizational success.

Incorporate practical and inventive strategies into your tax-filing routine, and regard tax season not as a stressful challenge but as an opportunity to boost your financial well-being. Safe travels, financial maestro, as you handle taxes skillfully and embark on a journey toward financial empowerment.

Conclusion

In closing, "How to Apply for Unemployment: Your Strategic Guide to Maximizing Unemployment Benefits" is not just a manual; it's a transformative conversation between kindred spirits navigating the challenging landscape of unemployment. Alex's journey, from the depths of uncertainty to the pinnacle of success, serves as a testament to the power of strategic thinking and Covey's timeless principles.

This literary gem goes beyond the bureaucratic intricacies of unemployment applications; it becomes a beacon of hope, urging readers to view unemployment not as a period of financial strain but as a canvas for painting a portrait of their future selves. The book is a roadmap to financial resilience, guiding readers through a mental shift, strategic intricacies, and the development of habits aligned with Covey's wisdom.

As we delve into the complexities of benefit applications, we simultaneously explore the development of habits that align with Covey's timeless principles. This guide is an invitation to embrace proactivity, prioritize what truly matters, and use the period of unemployment as a crucible for personal and professional transformation.

The incorporation of Covey's principles, such as "Begin with the End in Mind" and "Seek First to Understand, Then to Be Understood," adds depth to the narrative. It encourages readers not only to understand the bureaucratic maze but also to understand themselves—their strengths, values, and aspirations. This self-awareness becomes the foundation for a strategy that propels individuals toward a more fulfilling professional trajectory.

The guide acknowledges the emotional challenges of unemployment, emphasizing the importance of investing in empathy, effective communication, and resilience. It assures readers that, armed with strategic thinking and Covey's principles, they have the tools to navigate challenges with grace and purpose.

In the spirit of "Sharpen the Saw," the guide explores not only the practical aspects of benefit applications but also the holistic well-being that sustains individuals throughout the process. The chapters ahead offer strategies for maintaining physical, mental, and emotional well-being, recognizing that a resilient self is better equipped to weather the storms of change.

This guide is a collaborative exploration, with the author not just providing insights but walking alongside readers as a fellow traveler. Together, readers are invited to transcend the limitations of unemployment, emerging not just as beneficiaries of a system but as architects of their destinies.

May "How to Apply for Unemployment" be a beacon of empowerment, illuminating the path to not only claiming unemployment benefits but to claiming a future defined by resilience, purpose, and the unwavering belief that, in every challenge, there lies an opportunity for greatness. Welcome to a journey of strategic transformation—Thank you for reading "How to Apply for Unemployment: Your Strategic Guide to Maximizing Unemployment Benefits."

ONE LAST THING…

Thank you so much for reading this book. I poured a lot of sweat and tears into it.

Could you do me a favor? Please review this book on Amazon. Whether you thought it was great, terrible, or anywhere in between, I'd love to have your feedback.

Reviews are the best way for an author like me to get discovered. Readers like you can help make it happen.

Thanks in advance,

Kaitlin Henderson

www.ingramcontent.com/pod-product-compliance
Lightning Source LLC
Chambersburg PA
CBHW070915260726
48661CB00004B/1734